First World War
and Army of Occupation
War Diary
France, Belgium and Germany

38 DIVISION
Divisional Troops
Royal Army Medical Corps
129 Field Ambulance
1 December 1915 - 22 May 1919

WO95/2549/1

The Naval & Military Press Ltd
www.nmarchive.com
Published in association with The National Archives

Published by

The Naval & Military Press Ltd

Unit 10 Ridgewood Industrial Park,

Uckfield, East Sussex,

TN22 5QE England

Tel: +44 (0) 1825 749494

www.naval-military-press.com

www.nmarchive.com

This diary has been reprinted in facsimile from the original. Any imperfections are inevitably reproduced and the quality may fall short of modern type and cartographic standards.

© Crown Copyright
Images reproduced by permission of The National Archives, London, England, 2015.

Contents

Document type	Place/Title	Date From	Date To
Heading	WO/95/2549/1 129th Field Ambulance		
Heading	129th Field Ambulance Dec 1915-1919 May		
Heading	No 129 Field Ambulance Dec 15 Dec 18		
War Diary	Winchester	01/12/1915	01/12/1915
War Diary	Havre	02/12/1915	03/12/1915
War Diary	St Omer	04/12/1915	04/12/1915
War Diary	Clarques	05/12/1915	20/12/1915
War Diary	Calonne	21/12/1915	31/12/1915
Heading	War Diary 129th Field Ambulance R.A.		
War Diary	Calonne	01/07/1916	21/07/1916
War Diary	Zelobes	22/01/1916	19/02/1916
War Diary	Near Bethune	20/02/1916	29/02/1916
Heading	War Diary of OC 129th Field Ambulance		
War Diary	Near Bethune	01/03/1916	03/03/1916
War Diary	Near Bethune W. 30a.88 Bethune Combined Sheet.	04/03/1916	09/03/1916
War Diary	W 30 A 8.8.	10/03/1916	31/03/1916
Heading	War Diary of 129 Field Ambulance 38th (Welsh) Division from 1st April 1916 to 31st May 1916		
War Diary	Essars	01/04/1916	06/04/1916
War Diary	Essars White House	07/04/1916	14/04/1916
War Diary	Essars	15/04/1916	19/04/1916
War Diary	Lagorgue	20/04/1916	31/05/1916
Heading	War Diary of 129 Field Ambulance For June 1916		
War Diary	Lagorgue	01/06/1916	14/06/1916
War Diary	Marest Bailleul Aux Cornailles	15/06/1916	26/06/1916
War Diary	Ferme De Belleville Bernaville	27/06/1916	30/06/1916
War Diary	War Diary of No 129 Field Ambulance 38th (Welsh) Division from July 1st to July 31st 1916		
War Diary	Puchevillers	01/07/1916	01/07/1916
War Diary	Arqueves	02/07/1916	04/07/1916
War Diary	Ribemont	05/07/1916	05/07/1916
War Diary	Morlan Court	06/07/1916	12/07/1916
War Diary	Longpre	13/07/1916	13/07/1916
War Diary	Le Plouy	13/07/1916	13/07/1916
War Diary	Rubempre	14/07/1916	14/07/1916
War Diary	Couin	15/07/1916	29/07/1916
War Diary	Bois Du Warnimont	29/07/1916	30/07/1916
War Diary	Authieule	31/07/1916	31/07/1916
Heading	War Diary 129th Field Ambulance. 38th (Welsh) Division August 1916		
War Diary	Ferme Des 4 Cheminees Herzeel	01/08/1916	01/08/1916
War Diary	Watou	02/08/1916	20/08/1916
War Diary	Main Dressing Station A. 2.3.a.7.4	21/08/1916	31/08/1916
Heading	War Diary 129th Field Ambulance September 1916		
War Diary	Main Dressing Station A.2.3.C.2.9	01/09/1916	30/09/1916
War Diary	War Diary 129th Field Ambulance October 1916		
War Diary	A23.C.2.9	01/10/1916	31/10/1916
Heading	War Diary 129th Field Ambulance November 1916 Vol 9		
War Diary	A.23.C.29 Map. Sheet 28	01/11/1916	30/11/1916

Heading	War Diary 129th Field Ambulance December 1916 Vol 10		
War Diary	A23 C 2.9	01/12/1916	13/12/1916
War Diary	Watou K4 B.8.6 Sheet 27	14/12/1916	31/12/1916
Heading	War Diary 129th Field Ambulance January 1917 Vol XI		
War Diary	Watou K4 B 86 Sheet 27	01/01/1917	13/01/1917
War Diary	Proven F7b33 Sheet 27	14/01/1917	31/01/1917
Heading	War Diary 129th Field Ambulance February 1917 Vol 12		
War Diary	Proven F7b.3.3. 27	01/02/1917	28/02/1917
Heading	War Diary 129th Field Ambulance March 1917 Vol 13		
War Diary	Proven F7b.3.3 Sheet 27	01/03/1917	31/03/1917
Heading	War Diary 129th Field Ambulance April 1917 Vol 14		
War Diary	Proven F7b 3.3	01/04/1917	16/04/1917
War Diary	Wormhoudt C.1b C.6.7 Sheet 27	17/04/1917	30/04/1917
Heading	War Diary 129th Field Ambulance May 1917		
War Diary	Wormhoudt C.1b C 6.7 Sheet 27	01/05/1917	31/05/1917
Heading	War Diary 129th Field Ambulance for Month of June 1917		
Miscellaneous	B.E.F. Summary Of Medical War Diaries For 129th F.A. 38th Divn. 14th Corps, 5th Army. Western June 1917		
Miscellaneous	129th F.A. 38th Div. 14th Corps, 5th Army. O.C. Lt. Col. W.B. Edwards.		
Heading	B.E.F. Summary Of Medical War Diaries For 129th F.A. 38th Divn. 14th Corps, 5th Army. Western Front June 1917		
Miscellaneous	129th F.A. 38th Div. 14th Corps, 5th Army. O.C. Lt. Col. W.B. Edwards.		
War Diary	Wormhoudt C.1b C 6.7	01/06/1917	29/06/1917
War Diary	Ferme Der Longcourty W.21.b 7.8 Sheet 27	29/06/1917	30/06/1917
Heading	129th Field Ambulance War Diary July 1917 Vol 17		
War Diary	Auchy Au Bois	01/07/1917	14/07/1917
Miscellaneous	129th B.A. 38th Divn. 14th Corps, 5th Army: O.C. Lt. Col. W.B. Edwards.		
War Diary	129th B.A. 38th Divn. 14th Corps, 5th Army: O.C. Lt. Col. W.B. Edwards.		
Miscellaneous	129th F.A. 38th Div. 14th Corps, 5th Army. O.C. Lt. Col. W.B. Edwards.		
War Diary	Same	15/07/1917	15/07/1917
War Diary	Steenbecque	16/07/1917	16/07/1917
War Diary	Hondeghem	17/07/1917	17/07/1917
War Diary	Proven	18/07/1917	19/07/1917
War Diary	Coppernolle	20/07/1917	27/07/1917
War Diary	Sussex A.D.S. Sheet 28 C 19 C 2.6	27/07/1917	30/07/1917
War Diary	Sheet 28 C19c. 2.6	31/07/1917	31/07/1917
War Diary	C 19c26	31/07/1917	31/07/1917
Heading	War Diary 129 Field Ambulance August 1917 Vol 18		
Heading	B.E.F. Summary Of Medical War Diaries For 129th F.A., 38th Div., 14th Corps, 5th Army. Western Front Aug 1917		
War Diary	C19c 2.6 (Sheet 28)	01/08/1917	01/08/1917
War Diary	Canal Bank Sussex A D S C19 C 2.6	01/08/1917	05/08/1917
War Diary	Coppernolle	05/08/1917	06/08/1917
War Diary	Proven	06/08/1917	17/08/1917

Miscellaneous	B.E.F. 129th F.A. 38th Divn. 14th Corps, 5th Army. O.C. Lt. Col. W.H. Edwards.		
Miscellaneous			
Miscellaneous	129th F.A. 38th Divn. 14th Corps, 5th Army. O.C. Lt. Col. W.H. Edwards		
War Diary	Proven	18/08/1917	18/08/1917
War Diary	Pelissier Farm	18/08/1917	27/08/1917
War Diary	Gallwitz Farm Ads	27/08/1917	27/08/1917
War Diary	Solferino	27/08/1917	27/08/1917
War Diary	Gallwitz	27/08/1917	28/08/1917
War Diary	Solferino	28/08/1917	28/08/1917
War Diary	Gallwitz	28/08/1917	28/08/1917
War Diary	Solferino	28/08/1917	28/08/1917
War Diary	Pelissier Farm	28/08/1917	31/08/1917
Heading	War Diary 129 Field Ambulance September 1917 Vol 19		
Miscellaneous	B.E.F. Summary Of Medical War Diaries For 129th F.A., 38th Div., 14th Corps, 5th Army. Western Front Sept. 1917		
Miscellaneous			
War Diary	Pelissier Farm Nr Elverdinghe	01/09/1917	09/09/1917
War Diary	Pelissier Fm Nr Elverdinghe	10/09/1917	10/09/1917
War Diary	Singapore Camp Nr Proven	11/09/1917	14/09/1917
War Diary	Eecke Area	15/09/1917	15/09/1917
War Diary	Morbecque Area	16/09/1917	16/09/1917
War Diary	Le Nouveau Monde	16/09/1917	18/09/1917
War Diary	Nouveau Monde	19/09/1917	30/09/1917
Heading	War Diary 129th Field Ambulance October 1917 Vol 20		
War Diary	La Noveau Monde (G27c6.5 Sheet 36)	01/10/1917	05/10/1917
War Diary	La Noveau Monde	05/10/1917	16/10/1917
War Diary	Le Nouveau Monde (La Gorge)	17/10/1917	31/10/1917
Heading	War Diary 129 Field Ambulance. November 1917 Vol 21		
War Diary	Le Nouveau Monde (La Gorge)	01/11/1917	30/11/1917
Heading	War Diary. 129 Field Ambulance December 1917 Vol 22		
War Diary	Le Nouveau Monde (La Gorgue)	01/12/1917	31/12/1917
Heading	War Diary 129th Field Ambulance January 1918 Vol 23		
War Diary	Le Nouveau Monde (La Gorge)	01/01/1918	13/01/1918
War Diary	Vieux Berquin	13/01/1918	18/01/1918
War Diary	Guarbecque	19/01/1918	19/01/1918
War Diary	Norrent Fontes	20/01/1918	28/01/1918
Heading	War Diary 129 Field Ambulance. February 1918 Vol 24		
War Diary	Norrent Fontes	01/02/1918	13/02/1918
War Diary	Guarbecque	14/02/1918	14/02/1918
War Diary	Neuf Berquin	15/02/1918	15/02/1918
War Diary	Steenwerck	16/02/1918	17/02/1918
War Diary	Steenwerck	18/02/1918	28/02/1918
Heading	War Diary 129th Field Ambulance March 1918 Vol 25		
War Diary	Steenwerck	01/03/1918	20/03/1918
War Diary	Le Verrier	21/03/1918	30/03/1918
War Diary	Doulieu Area	31/03/1918	31/03/1918
Heading	War Diary 129 Field Ambulance April 1918 Vol 26		
War Diary	Doulieu	01/04/1918	01/04/1918
War Diary	Merville	02/04/1918	02/04/1918

War Diary	Mondecourt	02/04/1918	02/04/1918
War Diary	Herissart	02/04/1918	06/04/1918
War Diary	Rubempre	06/04/1918	11/04/1918
War Diary	Warloy	11/04/1918	29/04/1918
War Diary	Vadencourt	30/04/1918	30/04/1918
Heading	War Diary 129 Field Ambulance May 1918 Vol 27		
War Diary	Vadencourt	01/05/1918	06/05/1918
War Diary	Harponville	06/05/1918	20/05/1918
War Diary	Clairfaye	20/05/1918	31/05/1918
Heading	War Diary 129 Field Ambulance June 1918 Vol 28		
War Diary	Clairfaye	01/06/1918	04/06/1918
War Diary	Englebelmer	05/06/1918	08/06/1918
War Diary	Hedauville	09/06/1918	09/06/1918
War Diary	Clairfaye	10/06/1918	13/06/1918
War Diary	Englebelmer	14/06/1918	16/06/1918
War Diary	Clairfaye	17/06/1918	19/06/1918
War Diary	Englebelmer	20/06/1918	21/06/1918
War Diary	Clairfaye	21/06/1918	30/06/1918
Miscellaneous	Cover for Documents. Nature of Enclosures.		
Heading	War Diary of 129 Field Ambulance From 1st July 1918 To 31st July 1918		
War Diary	Site on Touten Court Lealvillers Road	01/07/1918	18/07/1918
War Diary	Herissart	19/07/1918	22/07/1918
War Diary	Valheureux	22/07/1918	30/07/1918
Heading	War Diary of 129 Field Ambulance From 1st August 1918 To 31st August 1918 Vol 30		
War Diary	Valheureux	01/08/1918	25/08/1918
War Diary	Clairfaye	25/08/1918	26/08/1918
War Diary	Hedauville	27/08/1918	29/08/1918
War Diary	Nr La Boiselle	29/08/1918	31/08/1918
Heading	129 Field Ambulance Original War Diary for month of September 1918 Vol 31		
War Diary	La Boiselle	01/09/1918	04/09/1918
War Diary	Beaulencourt	05/09/1918	05/09/1918
War Diary	Bazentin	06/09/1918	10/09/1918
War Diary	Rocquigny	11/09/1918	11/09/1918
War Diary	Fins	11/09/1918	20/09/1918
War Diary	Rocquigny	21/09/1918	21/09/1918
War Diary	Beaulencourt	22/09/1918	28/09/1918
War Diary	Heudecourt	29/09/1918	30/09/1918
Heading	War Diary of 129 Field Ambulance for month of October 1918 Vol 32		
War Diary	Heudicourt	01/10/1918	03/10/1918
War Diary	Epehy	04/10/1918	09/10/1918
War Diary	Villers Outreaux	10/10/1918	10/10/1918
War Diary	Clary	11/10/1918	12/10/1918
War Diary	Bertry	13/10/1918	25/10/1918
War Diary	Forest	26/10/1918	31/10/1918
Heading	War Diary of 129 Field Ambulance for month of November 1918 Vol 33		
War Diary	Forest	01/11/1918	05/11/1918
War Diary	Forest	01/11/1918	08/11/1918
War Diary	Locquignol	08/11/1918	30/11/1918
Heading	129 Field Ambulance Original War Diary for month of December 1918 Vol 34		
War Diary	Locquinol	01/12/1918	28/12/1918

War Diary	Inchy	29/12/1918	29/12/1918
War Diary	Warloy	30/12/1918	31/12/1918
Heading	129 Field Ambulance Original War Diary for month of January 1919 Vol 35		
War Diary	Warloy	01/01/1919	31/01/1919
Heading	129 Field Ambulance Original War Diary for month of February 1919 Vol 36		
War Diary	Warloy	01/02/1919	28/02/1919
Heading	129 Field Ambulance Original War Diary for month of March 1919 Vol 47		
Miscellaneous	On His Majesty's Service. O.C. 129th Field Amb.		
War Diary	Warloy-Baillon	01/03/1919	16/03/1919
War Diary	Lamotte Brebiere	17/03/1919	31/03/1919
Heading	129 Field Ambulance Original War Diary for month ending April 1919 Vol 38		
War Diary	Lamotte Brebiere	01/04/1919	30/04/1919
Heading	129 Field Ambulance Original War Diary for month of May 1919 Vol 39		
Miscellaneous	Cover for Documents. Nature of Enclosures.		
War Diary	Lamotte Brebiere	01/05/1919	22/05/1919

WO/95/2549/1

129th Field Ambulance

38TH DIVISION
MEDICAL

129TH FIELD AMBULANCE
DEC 1915 - ~~DEC 1918~~.
1919 MAY

No. 129 Field Ambulance.

Dec 15
Dec 18

WAR DIARY
INTELLIGENCE SUMMARY

Army Form C. 2118.

Place	Date	Hour	Summary of Events and Information	Remarks and references to Appendices
WINCHESTER	1.12.15	7.30 a.m	Left WINCHESTER for SOUTHAMPTON. Embarked on S.S. MANCHESTER IMPORTER	Appx 5TH
HAVRE	2.12.15	8.00 a.m	Disembarked at 4 p.m. arrived at No 5 REST CAMP, HAVRE at 10 p.m.	Appx LHG
HAVRE	3.12.15	10.89 p.m	Left HAVRE for ST OMER by train	Appx LHG
ST OMER	4.12.15	6 a.m	Marched to CLARQUES, where billeted	Appx HTK
CLARQUES	5.12.15		Sunday	Appx
Sd	6.12.15		Owing to form a divisional reserve station of 150 beds	Appx
Sd	7.12.15			Appx
Sd	8.12.15			Appx
Sd	9.12.15			Appx
Sd	10.12.15			Appx
Sd	11.12.15			Appx
Sd	12.12.15		Sunday	Appx
Sd	13.12.15			Appx
Sd	14.12.15			Appx
Sd	15.12.15			Appx

Mackenzie
Jan 1916

Army Form C. 2118.

WAR DIARY
or
INTELLIGENCE SUMMARY.
(Erase heading not required.)

Instructions regarding War Diaries and Intelligence Summaries are contained in F. S. Regs., Part II. and the Staff Manual respectively. Title pages will be prepared in manuscript.

Place	Date	Hour	Summary of Events and Information	Remarks and references to Appendices
CLARGUES	16.12.15		A section with Lt-Col SIMONS Lt REES and Lt BROWN sent to LAGORGUE, attached for instructions to 3rd Guards Sub-Division	Appx 1
Same	17.12.15		A section at LAGORQUE	Appx 2
Same	18.12.15		" " "	Appx 3
Same	19.12.15		" " " Snowy	Appx 4
Same	20.12.15		The Sub-Division moved to CALONNE	Appx 5
Same	21.12.15		A section at LAGORGUE	Appx 6
CALONNE	21.12.15		" " "	Appx 7
Same	22.12.15		" " "	Appx 8
Same	23.12.15		" " "	Appx 9
Same	24.12.15		" " "	Appx 10
Same	25.12.15		A section moves to CALONNE	Appx 11
Same	25.12.15		Christmas Day	Appx 12
Same	26.12.15		B Section with Lt PRYCE + Lt MENNIE to LOCON attached to Sqn. Field Ambulance for instruction Snowy	Appx 13
Same	27.12.15		B section at LOCON. Lt REES placed in charge of Brigade Wells at CALONNE	Appx 14
Same	28.12.15		" " "	Appx 15
Same	29.12.15		" " "	Appx 16
Same	30.12.15		" " "	Appx 17
Same	31.12.15		" " "	Appx 18

Robert Simons
Lt Col R.A.M.C.
O/C 3rd Sub-Division

War Diary.

129th Field Ambulance. R.A.

Jan 1916
Feb 1916

Army Form C. 2118.

WAR DIARY
or
INTELLIGENCE SUMMARY.
(Erase heading not required.)

Instructions regarding War Diaries and Intelligence Summaries are contained in F. S. Regs., Part II. and the Staff Manual respectively. Title pages will be prepared in manuscript.

Place	Date	Hour	Summary of Events and Information	Remarks and references to Appendices
CALONNE	1.1.16		B Section at LOCON returns to CALONNE	Ap. D & E.
Same	2.1.16		C Section with 2 Parry, Jones & Watkins to 9th Guards Field Ambulance at ESTAIRES In instruction	Ap. F. H.
Same	3.1.16		Ordered to establish Hospital In SCABIES at CALONNE. 6 ISO bed Hospital opened at the CHICORY MILL	Ap. L. H. Ap. I. J. Ap. L. L.
Same	4.1.16			Ap. L. L.
Same	5.1.16			
Same	6.1.16		B Section with Lts PRYCE & MENNIE to A.D.S. at RUE DE BOIS.	Ap. M. N.
Same	7.1.16		B Section at RUE DE BOIS.	Ap. O. P.
Same	8.1.16		" " " " " "	Ap. O. P.
Same	9.1.16		" " " " " "	Ap. Q. T.
Same	10.1.16		" " C Section with Lts PARRY, JONES & WATKINS returns from ESTAIRE.	Ap. L. S.

2353 Wt. W2544/1454. 700,000 5/15 D. D. & L. A.D.S.S./Forms/C. 2118.

Army Form C. 2118.

WAR DIARY
or
INTELLIGENCE SUMMARY.
(Erase heading not required.)

Place	Date	Hour	Summary of Events and Information	Remarks and references to Appendices
CALONNE	11.1.16		B Section at RUE DE BOIS	Mp 4424
Same	12.1.16		" " " " " "	Mp 4424
Same	13.1.16		" " " " " "	Mp 4424
Same	14.1.16		" " " " " "	Mp 4424
Same	15.1.16		" " " " " "	Mp 4424
Same	16.1.16		" Returned to CALONNE Lts PRYCE & MENNIE	Mp 4424
Same	17.1.16		" Returned to CALONNE	Mp 4424
Same	18.1.16			Mp 4424
Same	19.1.16		Lt JONES placed in charg of Rest Baths at VIEILLE CHAPELLE. Hunt goes to A.6.S. at KINGS ROAD Lt PARRY with 30 men of C Section to A.D.S.	Mp 407
Same	20.1.16		KINGS ROAD	Mp 4414
Same	21.1.16		The Field Ambulance moved to ZELOBES taking over buildings at R.27.C.1.4 from 5.8. Field Ambulance to form at Hospital for SCABIES cases	Mp 4430

2353 Wt W2544/I454 700,000 5/15 D.D.&L. A.D.S.S./Forms/C. 2118.

Army Form C. 2118.

Instructions regarding War Diaries and Intelligence
Summaries are contained in F. S. Regs., Part II.
and the Staff Manual respectively. Title pages
will be prepared in manuscript.

WAR DIARY
or
INTELLIGENCE SUMMARY.
(Erase heading not required.)

Place	Date	Hour	Summary of Events and Information	Remarks and references to Appendices
ZELOBES	22.1.16		C Section w/ Lt PARRY & JONES at KINGS ROAD.	
Same	23.1.16		" " " " " " " "	
Same	24.1.16		Capt Bush Board of Inquiry adj.	
Same	25.1.16		" " " " " "	
Same	26.1.16		Capt. Leas at 11.30 a.m. Inv. Inquiry	
Same	27.1.16		" " " " " "	
Same	28.1.16		" " " " " "	
Same	29.1.16		" " " " " "	
Same	30.1.16		" " " " " "	
Same	31.1.16		" " " " " "	

Army Form C. 2118.

WAR DIARY
or
INTELLIGENCE SUMMARY.
(Erase heading not required.)

Instructions regarding War Diaries and Intelligence Summaries are contained in F. S. Regs., Part II. and the Staff Manual respectively. Title pages will be prepared in manuscript.

Place	Date	Hour	Summary of Events and Information	Remarks and references to Appendices
ZELOBES	1.2.16		C Section at 16 PARRY & JONES at KINGS ROAD.	
Same	2.2.16		" " " " "	
Same	3.2.16		Capt WALSH RAMC laid up ill	
Same	4.2.16		Sister W.E. & L/C PARRY JONES & KINGS ROAD	
Same	5.2.16		" " " " "	
Same	6.2.16		" " " " "	
Same	7.2.16		" " " " "	
Same	8.2.16		" " " " "	
Same	9.2.16		" " " " "	
Same	10.2.16		Capt BURNE took a 10 day leave	
Same	11.2.16		" " " " "	
Same	12.2.16		" " " " "	
Same	13.2.16		" " " " "	

WAR DIARY
INTELLIGENCE SUMMARY.
(Erase heading not required.)

Army Form C. 2118.

Place	Date	Hour	Summary of Events and Information	Remarks and references to Appendices
ZELOBES	14.2.16		L/C PARRY & JONES with C Section at KINGS ROAD.	App XLT 19
Sau	15.2.16		" " " " " " " " "	App XLT 18
Sau	16.2.16		" " " " " " " " "	App XLT 19
Sau	17.2.16		C Section with L/C PARRY's returned to Zelobes	
			L/C MENNIE, 9 men & under cyclist reld over A.S. of LONE FARM	
			Handed over all Engineer Rolls except those of RICHEBOURG ST VAAST on a GRUB ST to 19" Division	No App
			LT JONES with 4 N.C.O.s + 18 men on KINGS ROAD	
			Cap. STEWART relvd 12 days Batt	App XX
Sau	18.2.16		LT JONES with 4 N.C.O.s + 15 men at KINGS ROAD	App XLI
			L/C MENNIE with 10 men at LONE FARM	

Army Form C. 2118.

WAR DIARY
or
INTELLIGENCE SUMMARY.
(Erase heading not required.)

Instructions regarding War Diaries and Intelligence Summaries are contained in F. S. Regs., Part II. and the Staff Manual respectively. Title pages will be prepared in manuscript.

Place	Date	Hour	Summary of Events and Information	Remarks and references to Appendices
ZELOBES	19.2.16		Lt BROWNE 20 men go to A.D.S at LONE FARM vi Lt MENNIE + 10 men	Mp L74
			Lt Col SIMONS, Capt WALSH & Lt REES WL 40 men proceed to WHITE HOUSE at W.30.a.8.8. BETHUNE - 4.00 PM had to open General Hospital Head quarter of the same at ZELOBES	Mp L69
Mea				
BETHUNE	20.2.16		Lt Col SIMONS Captain WALSH & Lt REES at WHITE HOUSE Capt BURKE & Lt PRYCE at ZELOBES Lt BROWNE + MENNIE at LONE FARM	
Sans	21.2.16		Surgeon General RIKE A.M.S visited Hospital at WHITE HOUSE + ZELOBES.	Mp L73 Mp L74
Sans	22.2.16		Lt General HAKING visited Hospital at ZELOBES.	Mp L74

2353 Wt. W2544/1454 700,000 5/15 D. D. & L. A.D.S.S./Forms/C. 2118.

Army Form C. 2118.

WAR DIARY
or
INTELLIGENCE SUMMARY.
(Erase heading not required.)

Place	Date	Hour	Summary of Events and Information	Remarks and references to Appendices
Mon BETHUNE	22.2.16		Capt BURKE evacuated from back	App 1/7
Sd	23.2.16		Visited CHATEAU BOIS DE PACAUT. will return to inspect hospital.	App 4/6
Sd	24.2.16			App 4/6
Sd	25.2.16			
Sd	26.2.16		Capt WALSH RAMC detailed for duty with 17th R.W.F.	App 4/4
Sd	27.2.16			App 4/4
Sd	28.2.16			App 4/6

Army Form C. 2118.

WAR DIARY
or
INTELLIGENCE SUMMARY.
(Erase heading not required.)

Instructions regarding War Diaries and Intelligence Summaries are contained in F. S. Regs., Part II. and the Staff Manual respectively. Title pages will be prepared in manuscript.

Place	Date	Hour	Summary of Events and Information	Remarks and references to Appendices
New BETHUNE	29.2.16		Lt. REES attached for duty with 1st R.W.F.	A/O 579

Robt. Nimmo
Lt.Col. R.A.M.C.
Off i/c Field Ambulance

Confidential

1243 Vol 2

War Diary

of

OC 129th Field Ambulance

3

38th Div

March 1916

Army Form C. 2118.

WAR DIARY
or
INTELLIGENCE SUMMARY.
(Erase heading not required.)

Place	Date	Hour	Summary of Events and Information	Remarks and references to Appendices
NCO/ BETHUNE	13.3.16		at WHITE HOUSE L/Col SIMONS, L/ JONES	
			at ZELOBES Capt BURKE & L/ PRYCE	
			at LONE FARM L/G BROWN, MENNIE	
			Capt STEWART returned from leave, reported sick,	
			at WHITE HOUSE, Taken to Hosp. at ZELOBES	Ap. 26
			Capt BURNE from ZELOBES to WHITE HOUSE.	Ap. 26
Same	2.3.16		ST DAVIDS DAY.	Ap. 26
Same	3.3.16			Ap. 26

Army Form C. 2118.

WAR DIARY
or
INTELLIGENCE SUMMARY.
(Erase heading not required.)

Place	Date	Hour	Summary of Events and Information	Remarks and references to Appendices
Near Ploegsteert W.30a.88 Point indicated	4.3.16		Lt R H SIMMONS Capt BURKE & Lt JONES at WHITEHOUSE with A section	Appx
			Capt STEWART & Lt PRYCE & 79 m— at ZELOBES	Appx
			Lt G BROWN & MENNIE at LONE FARM	Appx
Same	5.3.16		Sunday.	Appx
Same	6.3.16		A armed party B Lt PRYCE & 6 O.R. to ROBECQ	Appx
Same	7.3.16		Handed over ZELOBES to 106 Field Ambulance and pro ZELOBES to P29.6.6.3 (ROBECQ) Capt STEWART & L PRYCE & 79 O.R. B section	Appx
Same	8.3.16		Lt Col SIMMONS, Capt BURKE & Lt JONES at WHITEHOUSE with A section Capt STEWART & Lt PRYCE & B section at ROBECQ Lt BROWN & Lt MENNIE at LONE FARM	Appx
Same	9.3.16			Appx

Army Form C. 2118.

WAR DIARY
or
INTELLIGENCE SUMMARY.
(Erase heading not required.)

Instructions regarding War Diaries and Intelligence Summaries are contained in F. S. Regs., Part II. and the Staff Manual respectively. Title pages will be prepared in manuscript.

Place	Date	Hour	Summary of Events and Information	Remarks and references to Appendices
W30A B6	10.3.16			
Sa	11.3.16			
Sa	12.4.16			
Sa	13.4.16			
Sa	14.4.16			
Sa	15.4.16		Capt BURKE to LONE FARM	
			Lt. BROWN to WHITE HOUSE	
Sa	16.4.16		Lt. JONES to LONE FARM	
Sa	17.4.16		Lt. MENNIE to WHITE HOUSE	
Sa	18.4.16		Lt. REES return from ady. with 16.F Batt R.W.F.	
			Lt. MENNIE to ROBECQ	
			Lt. PRYCE start on leave	
Sa	19.4.16		Lt Col SIMONS, Lt BROWN + Lt REES to WHITE HOUSE	
			Capt STEWART + Lt MENNIE to ROBECQ	
			Capt BURKE + Lt JONES to LONE FARM	

2353 Wt. W2544/1454 700,000 5/15 D. D. & L. A.D.S.S./Forms/C. 2118.

Army Form C. 2118.

WAR DIARY
or
INTELLIGENCE SUMMARY.
(Erase heading not required.)

Instructions regarding War Diaries and Intelligence Summaries are contained in F. S. Regs., Part II. and the Staff Manual respectively. Title pages will be prepared in manuscript.

Place	Date	Hour	Summary of Events and Information	Remarks and references to Appendices

129/7 Kent
Vol 3

CONFIDENTIAL.

WAR DIARY

of

129 Field Ambulance
38th (Welsh) Division

from 1st April 1916
to 31st May 1916.

COMMITTEE FOR THE
MEDICAL HISTORY OF THE WAR
Date 31 AUG '15

Army Form C. 2118.

WAR DIARY
or
INTELLIGENCE SUMMARY.

(Erase heading not required.)

Instructions regarding War Diaries and Intelligence Summaries are contained in F. S. Regs., Part II. and the Staff Manual respectively. Title pages will be prepared in manuscript.

Place	Date	Hour	Summary of Events and Information	Remarks and references to Appendices
ESSARS	1/4/16		Captain BURKE R.A.M.C. will return to the station & report for duty with No 10 Field ambulance. Lt. REES will take over the A.D.S. at LONE FARM.	Appendix
S—	2/4/16			No xxx
Same	3/4/16		Captain PENNANT R.A.M.C. (New) for duty	No xxx
Same	4/4/16			No xxx
Same	5/4/16			No xxx
Same	6/4/16			No xxx
Same				

Army Form C. 2118.

WAR DIARY
or
INTELLIGENCE SUMMARY

(Erase heading not required.)

Instructions regarding War Diaries and Intelligence Summaries are contained in F. S. Regs., Part II. and the Staff Manual respectively. Title pages will be prepared in manuscript.

Place	Date	Hour	Summary of Events and Information	Remarks and references to Appendices
ESSARS	7.4.16		Lt Col SIMONS, Major BICKERTON & EDWARDS, Capt PENNANT & Lt TAYLOR at WHITE HOUSE. Lt REES & JONES at LONE FARM. CAPTAIN STEWART & Lt MENNIE at BOIS DE PACAUT.	Ap. A229
WHITEHOUSE			Lt MENNIE to relieve Capt PRYCE at W.2.8.b.o. 8 + 9.4.16.	
Same	8.4.16			Ap. A056
Same	9.4.16			Ap. A239
Same	10.4.16		Capt PENNANT to LONE FARM. Lt REES to WHITE HOUSE.	Ap. A40 Ap. A40
Same	11.4.16			
Same	12.4.16		Capt STEWART from BOIS DE PACAUT to LONE FARM. Lt JONES from LONE FARM to WHITE HOUSE. Lt REES from WHITE HOUSE to BOIS DE PACAUT.	Ap. A43
Same	13.4.16			
Same	14.4.16		Capt PENNANT from LONE FARM to WHITE HOUSE. Relieved on duty with No. 20 Auto Anti-gun, attack of it stuff it. Lt JONES to LONE FARM.	Ap. A46

Army Form C. 2118.

WAR DIARY
or
INTELLIGENCE SUMMARY.
(Erase heading not required.)

Place	Date	Hour	Summary of Events and Information	Remarks and references to Appendices
ESSARS	15.4.18			No Actof
Same	16.4.18		Lt TAYLOR to BOIS DE PACAUT. Lt REES to LAGORGUE to take over from 58 Div'l Band and 146 A.S M.B.	No Actof
Same	17.4.18		Lt JONES from LONE FARM to GREEN BARN. N.27.a.5.2. with N.C.O's & 'A' Section.	No Actof
Same	18.4.16		Capt. STEWART we had over A.D.S at LONE FARM to 133rd F.A. 2 N.C.O's & 20 men. Bearer Posn. of 133. 2 w/o Ambulances & stretcher posts at N.C.O's. & 20 men at A.D.S at GREEN BARN. Section one from BOIS DE PACAUT to 133rd F. Amb. at REGNIER LE CLERQ. 2 w/o Ambulance & relief over Head'q'rs WHITE HOUSE to 133rd Field Ambulance.	No Actof
Same	19.4.16		Prem'f staln at LAGORGUE from 58. 2 w/o Ambulances	No Actof
LAGORGUE	20.4.18		Lt Col SIMONS Maj EDWARDS, Lt REES, BROWNE, MENNIE & TAYLOR at LAGORGUE. Lt TAYLOR to be billeted at L.32.a.8.6. Capt STEWART & Lt JONES at GREEN BARN	No Actof
Same	22.4.18			No Actof
Same	23.4.18		Capt STEWART we have over the A.D.S at GREEN BARN to	No Actof

Army Form C. 2118.

WAR DIARY
or
INTELLIGENCE SUMMARY.
(Erase heading not required.)

Instructions regarding War Diaries and Intelligence Summaries are contained in F. S. Regs., Part II. and the Staff Manual respectively. Title pages will be prepared in manuscript.

Place	Date	Hour	Summary of Events and Information	Remarks and references to Appendices
LA GORGUE	23.4.16		2 W.O. ambulance of C. 35th Division joined the 130 F.O. ambulance. FLINQUE from the A.D.S. at LA	App 1 of 51
Same	24.4.16		Two relays company No. 2 D.S were sent as for duty at A.D.S. at GREENBARN front of EBENEZER and part	App 2 of 51
Same	25.4.16			App 3 of 51
Same	26.4.16			App 4 of 51
Same	27.4.16		Capt J.S. STEWART proceeded for duty with 51st Highland Division in C. Corps. 3rd Army & was attached to attached to to attached	No App
Same	28.4.16		Lt BROWNE to A.D.S at LA POINQUE	App 5 of 51
Same	29.4.16			App 6 of 51
Same	30.4.16			App 7 of 51

Robert L. Swan
Lieut Col R.A.M.C.
Brig. Field ambulance

Army Form C. 2118.

WAR DIARY
or
INTELLIGENCE SUMMARY.
(Erase heading not required.)

Instructions regarding War Diaries and Intelligence Summaries are contained in F. S. Regs., Part II. and the Staff Manual respectively. Title pages will be prepared in manuscript.

Place	Date	Hour	Summary of Events and Information	Remarks and references to Appendices
LAFORGUE	1/5/16		At LAFORGUE LtCol SIMONS Major EDWARDS, Lt REES, Lt MENATT Lt TAYLOR & Lt TAYLOR.	
Same	2/5/16		At LA FLINQUE Lt BROWNE & L JONES.	
Same	3.5.16			
Same	4.5.16		LtCol SIMONS graded Bn. from 4.5.16 to 14.5.16 Lt ME WIE to G.A.S. Lt JONES to own dressing station proceeded to 10.5.S.W.B. totally	
Same	5.5.16			
Same	6.5.16		Lt RIDDEL from 16th D.W.F. reported for duty	
Same	7.5.16			
Same	8.5.16		Lt T. McSELLA train	
Same	9.5.16		Lt T. McSELLA R reported for duty	
Same	10.5.16			
Same	11.5.16		Capt. R.C. WALLACE R.A.M.C. reported for duty	

Army Form C. 2118.

WAR DIARY
or
INTELLIGENCE SUMMARY.
(Erase heading not required.)

Instructions regarding War Diaries and Intelligence Summaries are contained in F. S. Regs., Part II. and the Staff Manual respectively. Title pages will be prepared in manuscript.

Place	Date	Hour	Summary of Events and Information	Remarks and references to Appendices
LA GORGUE	11.5.15			
Same	12.5.15			
Same	13.5.16		Capt REES R.A.M.C. proceeded on leave	
Same	14.5.16		Lt. T. M.C. SELLAR proceeded to C.O.S. for duty	
Same	15.5.16		Lt MINNIE returning to hospital for duty ~ proceeds thence to OMBRGS	
Same				
Same	16.5.16			
Same	17.5.16		L/Cpl N. VARLEY granted back pay from 17.5.16 to 27.5.16.	
Same	18.5.16		L/Cpl SIMONS returned from leave.	
Same	19.6.16			
Same	19.5.16		Capt WALLACE L proceed to C.O.S. for duty	
Same	20.6.16			
Same	21.5.16			
Same	22.5.16			

Army Form C. 2118.

WAR DIARY
or
INTELLIGENCE SUMMARY.

(Erase heading not required.)

Instructions regarding War Diaries and Intelligence Summaries are contained in F. S. Regs., Part II. and the Staff Manual respectively. Title pages will be prepared in manuscript.

Place	Date	Hour	Summary of Events and Information	Remarks and references to Appendices
IACOPOLE	23.5.16			
S—	24.5.16			
S—	25.5.16			
S—	26.5.16		Lt BROWNE R.A.M.C. in [?] to Bn from 26.5.16 & 5.6.16	
S—	27.5.16			
S—	28.5.16		Capt REES & Lt VARLEY return from Bn 28.5.16	
S—	29.5.16		Lt RIDDELL proceed to Bn 28.5.16.	
S—	30.5.16			
S—	31.5.16			

Lieut. J. Simons
2/ Col. D.A.D.M.S.
for H.Q. Brig. Ambulance
38 Division

2353 Wt. W2544/1454 700,000 5/15 D. D. & L. A.D.S.S./Forms/C. 2118.

Confidential

War Diary

of

129 Field Ambulance

for

June 1916

Army Form C. 2118.

WAR DIARY
or
INTELLIGENCE SUMMARY.
(Erase heading not required.)

Instructions regarding War Diaries and Intelligence
Summaries are contained in F. S. Regs., Part II.
and the Staff Manual respectively. Title pages
will be prepared in manuscript.

Place	Date	Hour	Summary of Events and Information	Remarks and references to Appendices
LABEOUF	1.6.16		Col McLean being relieved by Col SIMONS, Major EDWARDS, Capt WALLACE, Lt TAYLOR.	Appx
			at A.D.S. Lt SELLAR & Capt REES	
Same	2.6.16			Appx
Same	3.6.16			Appx
Same	4.6.16		Major MACKIE, Capt STOBIE & Lt MANUEL & Lt & 2 & RIVERS	Appx
			to 2/1 S. M. Foto ambulance & A Section for watchers	
Same	5/6/16		Capt STOBIE + 30 other ranks to A.D.S.	Appx
			Lt M'NUEL a tour of orderly duty at A.D. heavy station	
Same	6.6.16		Lt TAYLOR to G.D.S.	Appx
			Lt SELLAR to R.A. heavy station	
Same	7.6.16		Lt MANUEL & 28 other ranks to A.D.S.	Appx
			Capt STOBIE party return Hqrs a B S	
Same	8.6.16			Appx
Same	9.6.16			Appx

WAR DIARY or INTELLIGENCE SUMMARY

Army Form C. 2118.

Place	Date	Hour	Summary of Events and Information	Remarks and references to Appendices
LAGORGUE	10.5.16		Major MACKIE, Capt. 670 BIE, L. MANUEL & 2/2nd RIVERS & 2/1 S.M. Judo Albany & A Sellon Party engaged dam for B ambulance Sect. to St. John	
(same)	11.5.16		Capt. WALLACE D.A.D.C. dept. to take warrshop p to q. (Moore.) Capt. WELSH off. Lt. SELLAR dept to take into log p to 121st B.S. R.F.A. Reconno patu fm 2/3 S.M. field ambs. take over A.D.S. at LA FLINQUE EBENEZER FARM. Capt REES & Lt TAYLOR, C Sector, retn to LA FLINQUE	
(same)	12.6.16		Stable. Capt. REES return to LA FLINQUE dept LAGORGUE est 113 13.00 for GONNEHEM, L/Col SIMMONS, Major EDWARDS, Lt. BROWN, Lt. RIDDELL & Lt. TAYLOR.	
(same)	13.6.16		Capt. REES 13th went to GONNEHEM	
(same)	14.5.16		Amb. dept GONNEHEM for MAREST. L/Col SIMMONS, Major EDWARDS, Capt REES, Lt BROWN, RIDDELL & TAYLOR	

Army Form C. 2118.

WAR DIARY
or
INTELLIGENCE SUMMARY
(Erase heading not required.)

Instructions regarding War Diaries and Intelligence Summaries are contained in F. S. Regs., Part II. and the Staff Manual respectively. Title pages will be prepared in manuscript.

Place	Date	Hour	Summary of Events and Information	Remarks and references to Appendices
MAREST	15/6/16		Unit is at open war now MAREST for BAILLEUL AUX CORNAILLES. Took over dressing station from 75th Field Ambulance 2nd Division	No App 27
BAILLEUL AUX CORNAILLES	16.6.16		Field training	No App
Same	17.6.16		Field training	No App
Same	18.5.16		Field training	No App
Same	19.6.16		Field training. Lt BROWNE for company duty with 10th Middx Regt	App
Same	20.6.16		Field training. Lt SELLAR reported for duty from 12th R.D.A. Lt MENNIE returns to hospital	App
Same	21.6.16		Field training. Capt ANDREWS & Lt R JONES proceed for duty	App
Same	22.6.16		Field training	No App
Same	23.6.16		Field training	No App
Same	24.6.16		Aeroplane Field day	No App
Same	25.6.16		Divisional Field day	App
Same	26.6.16		Address given to Genl at BELLEVILLE	No App

WAR DIARY
INTELLIGENCE SUMMARY

Army Form C. 2118.

Place	Date	Hour	Summary of Events and Information	Remarks and references to Appendices
FERMÉ DE BELLEVUE	27.6.16		Ambulance moves to BERNAVILLE	Resp/[?]
BERNAVILLE	28.6.16		Lt. BROWNE rejoins from motor charge 10th队 S.W.B.	
"	29.6.16		Lt. R. JONES detached to motor charge of 16th Battn. R.W.F. Order of Tr. [?] A.D.M.S. & Lt. SELLAR detached in his place.	
"	30.		Ambulance O moves to PUCHEVILLERS	

Rees / Major
2 Lw B.O.M.C.
Or 129th Field Ambulance

Confidential

War Diary

of

No. 129 Field Ambulance.

38th (Welsh) Division

From July 1st to July 31st 1916

COMMITTEE FOR THE
MEDICAL HISTORY OF THE WAR
Date −9 OCT. 1916

Army Form C. 2118.

WAR DIARY
or
INTELLIGENCE SUMMARY.
(Erase heading not required.)

Instructions regarding War Diaries and Intelligence Summaries are contained in F. S. Regs., Part II. and the Staff Manual respectively. Title pages will be prepared in manuscript.

Place	Date	Hour	Summary of Events and Information	Remarks and references to Appendices
Pucheviller	1.7.16		Field Ambulance received orders to proceed to ARGUEVES. Personnel transferred as such to 64 Field Ambulance.	A/F
ARGUEVES	2.7.16	9.30am	Marched ARGUEVES. Lt TAYLOR R.A.M.C. attached for temporary duty with 131 Field Ambulance.	A/F
Same	3.7.16		Capt A.D. ANDREW proceeded for duty with No 5 Special Hosp at VILLERS BOCAGE. Capt. G.A. MEADEN reported for duty. Orders issued to proceed to RIBEMONT. Field Ambulance marched to RIBEMONT.	A/F
RIBEMONT	4.7.16	3am		A/F
	5.7.16		Orders to form two detachments to MORLANCOURT. To evacuate collecting station at L.9.a. & at 62.D. Trans. Took over Hospital at MORLANCOURT from 22nd Field Ambulance & the following Officers & 96 OR viz Major EDWARDS, Capt MEADEN Lt BROWNE & Lt MENNIE to remain behind with 1st Corps SIMONS, Capt REES, Lt RIDDELL, Lt JONES to MORLANCOURT	A/F

Army Form C. 2118.

WAR DIARY
or
INTELLIGENCE SUMMARY.
(Erase heading not required.)

Instructions regarding War Diaries and Intelligence Summaries are contained in F. S. Regs., Part II. and the Staff Manual respectively. Title pages will be prepared in manuscript.

Place	Date	Hour	Summary of Events and Information	Remarks and references to Appendices
MORLANCOURT	6.7.16		Lt BROWNE & 20 Other ranks from Advanced Collecting Station TOMORROW COURT.	M/O
Same	7.7.16		33 wounded admitted to evacy statn. 26 sick admitted to evacy statn. 89 men from Ambulance (ledgely attd) to MINDEN POST. 3 men from " " to CITADEL.	M/O
Same	8.7.16		32 N.C.Os etc from MORLANCOURT to MINDEN POST. 20 sick admitted to Evacy statn. 21 evacuated to 36 C.C.S.	M/O
Same	9.7.16		2Lt BROWN & JONES (Russ?) to MINDEN POST with 9 other ranks. 16 sick admitted to Evacy statn. 19 evacuated to 36 C.S.	M/O
Same	10.7.16		Lt RAYMOND JONES, R.A.M.C. killed in action near MAMETZ. Admitted to main dressing station 5 sick & 299 wounded, other ranks. Evacuated 196 wounded, other	M/O

2353 Wt. W2344/1454 700,000 5/15 D. D. & L. A.D.S.S./Forms/C. 2118.

WAR DIARY or INTELLIGENCE SUMMARY

Army Form C. 2118.

Place	Date	Hour	Summary of Events and Information	Remarks and references to Appendices
Saw	11.7.16		Number of patients admitted to Main Dressing Station Sick 23, wounded 177 other ranks. Evacuated to C.C.S. Wounded 286 other ranks.	N/D.
Saw	12.7.16		Major EDWARDS, Capt. MEADEN, Lt. BROWN & Lt. MENNIE with tent of unit returned from the old collecting station & MINDEN POST to MORLANCOURT. Handed over main Dressing Station at MORLANCOURT to 22nd Field Ambulance. Hospital admissions Sick 2, wounded 3. Ad hoc transport lorries Divisional Train at 1.30 p.m. at MOR- LANCOURT. hen Lt. MENNIE for VAUCHELLES-LES-QUESNOY. Lt.Col. SIMONS, major EDWARDS Capt. REES, Capt. MEADEN & Lts. RIDDELL & Lt. QM. VARLEY left MORLANCOURT for LONGPRE at EDGE HILL & entrained at 4.15 p.m. with 7 other ranks. Lt. BROWN & 100 other ranks remaining at MORLAN- COURT.	
LONGPRE	12.7.16.4.15p.m.			
LONGPRE	13.7.16.19a.m.		Remainder of LONGPRE & proceeded on foot to AILLY & LE PLOUY. Road: LE PLOUY at 9.30 a.m. Orders received to have LE PLOUY	N/D

Army Form C. 2118.

WAR DIARY
or
INTELLIGENCE SUMMARY.
(Erase heading not required.)

Instructions regarding War Diaries and Intelligence Summaries are contained in F. S. Regs., Part II. and the Staff Manual respectively. Title pages will be prepared in manuscript.

Place	Date	Hour	Summary of Events and Information	Remarks and references to Appendices
LE PLOUY	13.7.16		at 3.30 p.m. by motor char-à-banc for RUBEMPRE. arrived at RUBEMPRE at 11.45 p.m. having flown Lt MENNIE & horse transport	h/o
RUBEMPRE	14.7.16		Left RUBEMPRE at 1.46 p.m. arriving at COVIN at 6.30 p.m. Lt RIDDELL & 13 other ranks proceed to take over the advanced dressing station at HEBUTERNE from 1/3 North Midland Field Ambulance	h/o
COVIN	15.7.16		Took over dressing station at COVIN from 1/3 South Midland Field Ambulance at 12 noon. Capt MEADEN & 12 other ranks proceeded to HEBUTERNE to take charge R.A.S.S. Lt W.O. WELPLY R.A.M.C reported for duty. Lt BROWN & 100 other ranks reported unit. Hospital admissions Sick 19 wounded 1 transfers for 1/3 South Midland Field Ambulance sick 5, wounded 4, evacuated 1 officer wounded, 3 other ranks wounded	h/o
Same	16.7.16		Lt W.O. WELPLY R.A.M.C transferred to 131/1 Field Ambulance for duty. Lt H.R. HORTER R.A.M.C reported for duty	h/o

WAR DIARY or INTELLIGENCE SUMMARY

Army Form C. 2118.

Place	Date	Hour	Summary of Events and Information	Remarks and references to Appendices
Sans	16.7.16		Admitted & Evacuated Officers sick 2; other ranks 16 sick 10 wounded. Evacuated to C.C.S. Officers sick 2; other ranks 3 sick. Discharged to duty other ranks 11 sick.	M.O.
Sans	17.7.16		Lt TAYLOR R.A.M.C. reported for duty on return from 131 F.Amb. Admitted 1 N.C.O. & 70 men attached for duty self same day sick. Hospital admissions 19 O/R, 2 wounded. Evacuated to C.C.S. 6 sick. Duty 2 O/R 1 wounded	M.O.
Sans	18.7.16		One N.C.O. & 14 men proceeded to A.D.S.S. at HEBUTERNE. Hospital admissions Officer wounded 1. other ranks 36 sick 2 wounded. Evacuated to C.C.S. Officer wounded 1. other ranks 6 sick 2 wounded. other ranks 3 sick. other ranks 14 sick. Corp. Ross Stokes.	M.O.

Army Form C. 2118.

WAR DIARY
or
INTELLIGENCE SUMMARY.
(Erase heading not required.)

Place	Date	Hour	Summary of Events and Information	Remarks and references to Appendices
Som	19.7.16		Hospital admissions Officers sick 3 wounded nil	
			" " Other ranks " 14 " 4	
			" " Officers sick 1 " nil	
			Evacuated to C.C.S. Other ranks " 5 " 6	Ab
			Transfers to 138 F.A. Other ranks sick 17	
			" to Brit Australia Other ranks sick 12 wounded 3	
Som	20.7.16		1 N.C.O. & 19 men proceeded for duty to 123 Field Co R.E. to supersede	
			a body supplied	
			Hospital admissions Officers sick nil wounded nil	
			" " Other ranks " 19 " 4	
			" " " " 2 " 4	
			Evacuated to C.C.S. " " 11 " 11	
			Transfers to Brit N.S. " " 18 " 2	MD.

WAR DIARY
or
INTELLIGENCE SUMMARY.

(Erase heading not required.)

Army Form C. 2118.

Place	Date	Hour	Summary of Events and Information	Remarks and references to Appendices
Some	26/7/16		Admission to Hospital Officers Sick and Wounded 2	
			" " " Other rank " " 20	
			Evacuated to C.C.S " " " 10	
			Transferred to Sub. N.S " " " 8	
			" 130 F.A. " Sick cases 5.	M.
Same	27/7/16		Admission to Hospital Officers Sick and Wounded 3	
			" " " O.R. " " 16	
			Evacuation to C.C.S Officers " " 1	
			" " O.R. " " 1	
			" " O.R. " " 6	
			Transferred to Sub. Hospital O.R " " 1	
Same	28/7/16		Admission to Hospital Officers " " 4 " " 2	M.
			" " O.R. " " 37 " " 6	

WAR DIARY
or
INTELLIGENCE SUMMARY
(Erase heading not required.)

Army Form C. 2118.

Place	Date	Hour	Summary of Events and Information	Remarks and references to Appendices
Sand	23/7/16		Evacuation to C.C.S. Officers S.U. – N/S Wounded 2	
			" " O.R. " 3	
			Transferred to But Hospital O.R. 9 " 4	
			Transferred to 131 C.C.S. O.B.&R. Officers deputies. N/S in 2	
			O.R. 9	
			Transferred to 130 F.A.B.C. O.R. Other Services 2	
			Handed over command of 129th Field Ambulance to Major	N/O.
Sand	24/7/16		W. BICKERTON EDWARDS. R.A.M.C. with all stores, transport, documents & accounts, will balance of men in hand.	N/O.
			Bhu[...] Lt Col R.A.M.C.	

Army Form C. 2118.

WAR DIARY
or
INTELLIGENCE SUMMARY.

(Erase heading not required.)

Place	Date	Hour	Summary of Events and Information	Remarks and references to Appendices
Same	24.7.16.	8-30pm.	Took over charge of the 129th Field Ambulance from Lt. Col. ROBERT J. SIMONS. R.A.M.C. with all stores, transport, armaments and balance of money in hand as shown in handing over certificates.	
			Sick Wounded	
			Admission to Hospital Officers 2 —	
			O.R. 39 12	
			Evacuated to C.C.S Officers 2 —	
			O.R. 10 13	
			Transferred to M.R.S. O.R. 8 —	
			Discharged to Duty Officers 1 —	
			O.R. 1 —	
			W. Bickerton Edwards	

Army Form C. 2118.

WAR DIARY
or
INTELLIGENCE SUMMARY.
(Erase heading not required.)

Instructions regarding War Diaries and Intelligence Summaries are contained in F.S. Regs., Part II. and the Staff Manual respectively. Title pages will be prepared in manuscript.

Place	Date	Hour	Summary of Events and Information	Remarks and references to Appendices
Same	25/7/16		Sergt Major BOLLAND reported himself for duty and was taken on the strength of the 129th Field Ambulance	
			Admission to Hospital	
			Officers Sick Wounded	
			2 nil	
			O.R. 21 8	
			Evacuated to C.C.S. officers nil	
			O.R. 2 6	
			Transferred to D.R.S. O.R. 25 7	D.R.S.
Same	26/7/16		Corpl LEWIS and 19 men returned to this station from fatigue Duty with 123rd Field Co R.E. at SAILLY DELL	

Army Form C. 2118.

WAR DIARY
or
INTELLIGENCE SUMMARY.
(Erase heading not required.)

Instructions regarding War Diaries and Intelligence Summaries are contained in F. S. Regs., Part II. and the Staff Manual respectively. Title pages will be prepared in manuscript.

Place	Date	Hour	Summary of Events and Information	Remarks and references to Appendices
Same	26/7/16		Admission to Hospital Officers Sick 3 wounded nil	W.S.3.
			O.R. 27 3	
			Evacuated to C.C.S. Officers Sick 3 wounded	
			O.R. 1 1	
			Transferred to D.R.S O.R. 11 nil	
			,, ,, 130 Field Amb. 1 (also wounded) nil	
			Discharged Duty O.R. 2 nil	

Army Form C. 2118.

WAR DIARY
or
INTELLIGENCE SUMMARY.
(Erase heading not required.)

Place	Date	Hour	Summary of Events and Information	Remarks and references to Appendices
Same	27/7/16		Received R.A.M.C order No 17 by A.D.M.S 38 WELSH DIVISION with reference r/ships at Main Dressing Station at COUIN and advanced Dressing Station at HEBUTERNE on afternoon of 28.7.16 and to proceed to BOIS DU WARNIMONT on morning of 29.7.16 and continue theirs until receipt of further orders.	
			sick wounded	
			Hospital. Admitted O.Ranks sitting 24 3	
			dying 1	
			Evacuations C.C.S	
			Officers sitting nil nil	
			dying 1 nil	
			O.Ranks sitting 6 3	
			dying 2 3	
			" D.R.S. O.Ranks. 11	

WAR DIARY
or
INTELLIGENCE SUMMARY.

Army Form C. 2118.

Place	Date	Hour	Summary of Events and Information	Remarks and references to Appendices
Same	27.7.16		Hospital Transferred 130th Field Ambulance Sick O. Ranks 2 Discharged Duty Officers 1 O. Ranks 1	M.R.E.

Same	28.7.16		Handed over MAIN DRESSING at COUIN at 4 p.m. to 62nd FIELD AMBULANCE. Remained in Billets at this Sequel to the night 28/29-7-16
			
			Hospital State
			Admitted Officers sitting sick 1 wounded nil
			                            dying nil nil
			          O. Ranks sitting 11 nil
			                  dying 1 nil
			Transferred from 130 Field Amb sitting 8 —	

Army Form C. 2118.

WAR DIARY
or
INTELLIGENCE SUMMARY.
(Erase heading not required.)

Instructions regarding War Diaries and Intelligence Summaries are contained in F. S. Regs., Part II. and the Staff Manual respectively. Title pages will be prepared in manuscript.

Place	Date	Hour	Summary of Events and Information	Remarks and references to Appendices
Somme	28.7.16		Evacuations C.C.S. O. Ranks. Sick 16 wounded 2	
			Sitting	
			Lying 3 2	
			Sitting 35 8	
			Transferred D.R.S.	
			130th Field Amb. Sitting 2 —	
			" 62nd Field Amb Officers 4 —	
			O. Ranks. 63 3	W.B.8
			Transferred to 62nd Field Amb and marched to Bois DLL WARNIMONT	
Somme	29.7.16		left site at COUIN at 9-45 A.M.	
			arriving here at 11-15 A.M.	
			A.D.S at HEBUTERNE handed over to 65th Field Ambulance.	
			at 9 A.M. Capt. MEADEN with main RIDDEL and party from	
			at 9 A.M. joined main body.	
BOIS DU WARNIM			A.D.S rejoined main body.	
-ONT			Received RAMC order no 18 by A.D.M.S 38th WELSH DIVISION dated	

Army Form C. 2118.

WAR DIARY
or
INTELLIGENCE SUMMARY.
(Erase heading not required.)

Instructions regarding War Diaries and Intelligence Summaries are contained in F. S. Regs., Part II. and the Staff Manual respectively. Title pages will be prepared in manuscript.

Place	Date	Hour	Summary of Events and Information	Remarks and references to Appendices
Same	29.7.16		Bivouacked at BOIS DU WORNIMONT for night 29/30.7.16	
Same	30.7.16	2 A.M.	Received at 2 A.M. 113 Brigade operation order no 67 dated 29.7.16 with reference to entrainment. At TAYLOR R.A.M.C. and one N.C.O. and two men proceed in charge of two Motor Ambulances to detraining point of 113 Brigade at HOPOUTRE at 9 A.M. Unit left BOIS DU WORNIMONT at 9-40 A.M. passing through THIEVRES at 11-45 A.M. and arrived at AUTHIEULE at 2-30 P.M.	W.B.E.
AUTHIEULE	31.7.16		left AUTHIEULE at 8-15 A.M. Unit entrained at DOULLENS station at 11-30 A.M. left DOULLENS (north station) at 12-15 P.M. and arrived at HOPOUTRE station at 6-30 A.M.	W.B.E.

Confidential

Vol 6

ORIGINAL
WAR DIARY

129th Field Ambulance.
38th (Welsh) Division

August 1916.

WAR DIARY
or
INTELLIGENCE SUMMARY.

(Erase heading not required.)

Army Form C. 2118.

Place	Date	Hour	Summary of Events and Information	Remarks and references to Appendices
Ferme des 4 CHEMINEES HERZEEL	1.8.16		Unit arrived at Ferme des 4 CHEMINEES from Railhead HOPOUTRE at 12-15 A.M. Dr THOMAS KELLY R.A.M.C taken on the strength of this Unit as and from 1.8.16 Sick Hospital admitted O.Ranks 9	W.13.2
WATOU	2.8.16		Unit left HERZEEL on the morning of the 2?.8-16 arriving at WATOU (HOSPICE DES VIEILLARD) at 11-15 A.M. Hospital admitted Sick O.R. 11 Evacuated C.C.S. 3 O.R. 3	W.B.3
Same	3.8.16		1 N.C.O and 7 men proceeded to baths at COUTHOVE for duty. Sick Hospital admitted O.R. 3 Evacuated C.C.S. 2 Discharged to Duty 1	W.B.6

2353 Wt. W2544/1454 700,000 5/15 D. D. & L. A.D.S.S./Forms/C. 2118.

Army Form C. 2118.

WAR DIARY
or
INTELLIGENCE SUMMARY.
(Erase heading not required.)

Instructions regarding War Diaries and Intelligence Summaries are contained in F. S. Regs., Part II. and the Staff Manual respectively. Title pages will be prepared in manuscript.

Place	Date	Hour	Summary of Events and Information	Remarks and references to Appendices
Same	4.8.16		Hospital Admitted . Sick 5	
			O.R.	
			Evacuated CCS. 3 Sitting	
			Duty 2	W118
Same	5.8.16		Capt MEADEN R.A.M.C. proceeded on leave	
			Hospital Admitted Sick 5	
			Transferred D.R.S. 4	W118
Same	6.8.16		Hospital Admitted sick 4	
			Transfr. to D.R.S. 5	W118

WAR DIARY
or
INTELLIGENCE SUMMARY.
(Erase heading not required.)

Army Form C. 2118.

Place	Date	Hour	Summary of Events and Information	Remarks and references to Appendices
Same	7.8.16		Hospital Admitted Sick 2	W.B.E.
			O.R. 2	
			Transferred to D.R.S. 3	
			Evacuated to C.C.S. 3	
Same	8.8.16		Hospital Admitted 4	W.B.
			O.R. 2	
			Transferred to D.R.S. 3	
			Evacuated to C.C.S. 3	
Same	9.8.16		Hospital O.R. 4 wounded	W.B.E.
			Transferred to D.R.S. 5 1	
			Evacuated to C.C.S. 1	

WAR DIARY
or
INTELLIGENCE SUMMARY.
(Erase heading not required.)

Army Form C. 2118.

Place	Date	Hour	Summary of Events and Information	Remarks and references to Appendices
Somme	10.8.16		Hospital O.R. Admitted — sick 6 Evacuated C.C.S. 1 To Duty 1	WR5.
Somme	11.8.16		Lt Thos. KELLY R.A.M.C. proceeded to １/15 14 WELCH Regt on temporary duty as M.O. to that Regt Hospital — sick 4 Admitted 4 Transferred to D.R.S. 4	WR5.
Somme	12.8.16		Hospital — sick 8 Admitted 4 Trans to D.R.S 3 Evacuated to C.C.S	WR5

WAR DIARY or INTELLIGENCE SUMMARY.

Army Form C. 2118.

(Erase heading not required.)

Place	Date	Hour	Summary of Events and Information	Remarks and references to Appendices
Same	13.8.16		Hospital Admitted Sick O.R. 7 wounded 1 Evacuated to C.C.S 1	W.B.2.
Same	14.8.16		Hospital Admitted Sick O.R. 7 Evacuated to C.C.S 4 Transferred to D.R.S 1 Lt. D.R. TAYLOR R.A.M.C proceeded for temporary duty as M.O. to 122 R.F.A at LEDRINGHEM	W.B.3.
Same	15.8.16		Hospital Admitted Sick O.R. 6 Evacuated to C.C.S. 6 Transferred D.R.S 1	W.B.2.

WAR DIARY
or
INTELLIGENCE SUMMARY.
(Erase heading not required.)

Army Form C. 2118.

Place	Date	Hour	Summary of Events and Information	Remarks and references to Appendices
Same	16.8.16		Hospital Admitted Sick 3	W788
			O.R. 3	
			Evacuated to C.C.S. 3	
			Transferred to D.R.S. 3	
Same	17.8.16		Hospital Admitted Sick 3	W788
			O.R. 3	
			Evacuated to C.C.S 3	
			Transferred D.R.S 1	
			Discharged Duty	
Same	18.8.16		Hospital Admitted Sick 2	W788
			O.R. 4	
			Evacuated to C.C.S. 7	
			Transferred D.R.S. 2	
			Discharged - Duty	

WAR DIARY or INTELLIGENCE SUMMARY.

Army Form C. 2118.

(Erase heading not required.)

Place	Date	Hour	Summary of Events and Information	Remarks and references to Appendices
Same	19.8.16		Hospital Admitted Sick O.R. 4 Evacuated to C.C.S. 2 Discharged Duty 1	
			Lt. BROWNE. R.A.M.C. together with Lt. MENNIE. R.A.M.C. one Sergeant and 13 (Thirteen) men proceeded as advanced party to A.D.S. at ESSEX FARM C.19.c.2.4 & the A.D.S. at SUSSEX FARM. C.19.c.0.8.	WJR8
			Lt. RIDDELL. R.A.M.C. together with 10 men proceeded as an advanced party to the Main Dressing Station at A.23.A.7.4. "Sheet 28"	
Same	20.8.16		Capt. F.T. REES. R.A.M.C with 3 N.C.O. + 20 men proceeded to the Main dressing Station at A.23.A.7.4. Lt. RIDDELL R.A.M.C together with 1 N.C.O + 23 proceeded to take over the advanced dressing stations at ESSEX & SUSSEX Farms. Hospital Admitted Sick O.R. 8 Evacuated to C.C.S. 3 Lt. BROWNE. R.A.M.C. returned to Main dressing station at A.23.A.7.4 at midnight	WJR8

WAR DIARY
INTELLIGENCE SUMMARY

Army Form C. 2118.

Place	Date	Hour	Summary of Events and Information	Remarks and references to Appendices
Main Dressing Station A.23.a.7.4	21.8.16		Major W. BICKERTON EDWARDS. R.A.M.C. together with Lt. HURTER and main body of 129 Field Ambulance proceeded 16 Main dressing station at A.23.a.7.4 where they arrived at midday and took over the hospital from the XIth Field Ambulance, 4th Division. Capt C.A. MEADEN R.A.M.C reported for duty on returning from leave. Lt. W. BROWNE proceeded to England to report at the WAR OFFICE	
			Hospital Admitted Sick Wounded	
			Officers 0 0	
			Other Ranks 6 5	
			Transferred from 11th Field Ambulance, other ranks sick 4.	
Same	22/8/16		Hospital admitted Sick Wounded	
			Officers 1 0	
			Other Ranks 13 6	
			Wounded O.R.S other ranks 3 3	
			Col GERRARD D.D.M.S VIII Corps visited Field Ambulance.	

WAR DIARY
or
INTELLIGENCE SUMMARY.

(Erase heading not required.)

Army Form C. 2118.

Place	Date	Hour	Summary of Events and Information	Remarks and references to Appendices
Same	23/8/16		Hospital admitted. Sick Wounded Officer 0 1 Other Ranks 12 4 Evacuated C.C.S. Other Ranks 3 1 Transferred D.R.S. Other Ranks 4 0 Transferred to 130th Field Ambulance Other Ranks 2 0 Major W. Bitherton EDWARDS, R.A.M.C. granted 7 days leave 24/8/16 to 31/8/16. Major J.C. DAVIES. R.A.M.C. took over temporary command	✓
Same	24/8/16		Hospital admitted Sick Wounded Other Ranks 12 4 Evacuated C.C.S. 4 Other Ranks Transferred to D.R.S. 6 3 Other Ranks Transferred to 130th Field Ambulance Other Ranks 2 0 Attached to duty Other Ranks 2. to A.D.S. for duty on a working party. 6 additional men proceeded to A.D.S. for duty on a working party.	✓

Army Form C. 2118.

WAR DIARY
or
INTELLIGENCE SUMMARY.
(Erase heading not required.)

Place	Date	Hour	Summary of Events and Information	Remarks and references to Appendices
Somme	25/7/16		Hospital Sick Wounded	
			Admitted	
			Officers 2 0	
			Other Ranks 14 15	
			Evacuated to C.C.S.	
			Officers 0 1	
			Other Ranks 1 3	
			Transfer to D.R.S.	
			Other Ranks 5 1	
			Discharged to Outposts	
			Other Ranks 1 0	RD/
			Col. F. INGORAM. ADMS 35th DIVISION visited Field Ambulance.	
	26/7/16		Hospital Sick Wounded	
			Admitted	
			Officers 0 6	
			Other Ranks 8	
			Evacuated to C.C.S.	
			Officers 2 0	
			Other Ranks 6 4	
			Transfer to D.R.S.	
			Other Ranks 4 10	
			Discharged to Duty	
			Other Ranks 1 0	
			Lieut TAYLOR. D.R. RAMC attach M. Strength of Unit, & posted in pursuance A.M.O. to 122 R.F.A.	

Army Form C. 2118.

WAR DIARY
or
INTELLIGENCE SUMMARY.
(Erase heading not required.)

Instructions regarding War Diaries and Intelligence Summaries are contained in F. S. Regs., Part II. and the Staff Manual respectively. Title pages will be prepared in manuscript.

Place	Date	Hour	Summary of Events and Information	Remarks and references to Appendices
Same	27/8/16		Hospital. admitted Sick Wounded	
			Officers 0 1	
			Other Ranks 20 7	
			Evacuated C.C.S.	
			Officers 0 1	
			Other Ranks 6 8	
			Transferred S.A.S.	
			Officers 1 0	
			Other Ranks 5 2	
			Discharged Duty	
			Officers 0 0	
			Other Ranks 1	
			Capt L. L. HADLEY R.A.M.C. posted to camp from 28/8/16 to 11/9/16 on renewal of contract.	
			Capt MEADEN C.A. R.A.M.C. directed to take medical & sanitary charge of :-	
			123 C° R.E. at C 26-d.2.1.	
			124 C° R.E. at C 19 c.2.3. Hut 28 40.000	R
			135 C° R.E. at C 23-c.10.5	
			Div TMB at { C 13 a.0.6 / C 25 - a.2.1. }	
Same	28/8/16		Hospital. Sick Wounded	
			admitted	
			Other ranks 12 5	
			Evacuated C.C.S. Other ranks 2 3	
			Officers 1 DR 3 W 3 1	
			Discharged Duty M 0	R

Army Form C. 2118.

WAR DIARY
or
INTELLIGENCE SUMMARY.
(Erase heading not required.)

Instructions regarding War Diaries and Intelligence Summaries are contained in F. S. Regs., Part II. and the Staff Manual respectively. Title pages will be prepared in manuscript.

Place	Date	Hour	Summary of Events and Information	Remarks and references to Appendices
Same	29/8/16		Hospital admitted Sick Wounded.	
			Other ranks 19 2	
			Evacuated C.C.S. 3	
			Evacuated to Special Hospital BOESCHEPE	
			Other ranks 1. (Self inflicted wound).	
			Transferred to C.R.S	
			Other ranks 1 0	
			Officer 1	
			Transferred to D.R.S.	
			Other ranks 4	
			Officer 1	
			Discharged to duty 1 0	
			Other ranks	
				JR/
Same	30/8/16		Lieut KELLY T. R.A.M.C. reported sick from 16th Batt. Welsh Regiment	
			Sick Wounded	
			Hospital admitted Officer 1 0	
			Other ranks 9 1.	
			Evacuated to C.C.S.	
			Officer 1 0	
			Other ranks 4 1.	
			Transferred to D.R.S 5 4.	
			Other ranks	
			Transferred to 131st Field ambulance (AR) 5	
			(CR) 2	
			Discharged to duty 2 0	JR/

Army Form C. 2118.

WAR DIARY
or
INTELLIGENCE SUMMARY.
(Erase heading not required.)

Instructions regarding War Diaries and Intelligence Summaries are contained in F. S. Regs., Part II. and the Staff Manual respectively. Title pages will be prepared in manuscript.

Place	Date	Hour	Summary of Events and Information	Remarks and references to Appendices
Somme	30/8/16		Lieut KELLY T. RAMC granted leave from 30/8/16 to 13/9/16 on account of contract	
	31/8/16		Hospital admitted Ach Wounded	
			Officers 1 0	
			Other ranks 8 2	
			Evacuated to C.C.S.	
			Other ranks 2 2	
			Transferred D.R.S.	
			Other ranks 7 0	
			Discharged to duty	
			Other ranks 1 0	109
			MAJOR W. BICKERTON EDWARDS. R.A.M.C. assumed to the temporary rank of LIEUT. COLONEL whilst commanding 129' Field Ambulance.	
			LIEUT. TAYLOR. R.A.M.C. is taken on Strength of 129 Field Ambulance	

J C Burns Major R.A.M.C.
O/C 129' Field Ambulance
38 (West) Division

ORIGINAL
140/1734

COMMITTEE FOR THE
MEDICAL HISTORY OF THE WAR
Date 30 OCT 1916

38th Div

WAR DIARY
129th Field Ambulance
SEPTEMBER 1916.

Confidential
Sept 1916

Army Form C. 2118.

WAR DIARY
or
INTELLIGENCE SUMMARY.

(Erase heading not required.)

Place	Date	Hour	Summary of Events and Information	Remarks and references to Appendices
Main Dressing Station A23.C.2.9.	1.9.16		Lt-Col Edwards. R.A.M.C. returned from leave. Major DAVIES. R.A.M.C. returned 131st FIELD AMBULANCE, Lt D.R.TAYLOR. R.A.M.C. proceeded on a three days course of instruction in Gas to OXELAERE.	
			Hospital admitted. Sick wounded	
			O.R. 29 10	
			Evacuated C.C.S. O.R. 3 6	
			Transferred D.R.S. 5 nil	W.B.E.
			Hospital admitted – 1	
	2.9.16		O.R. 7 3	
			Evacuated C.C.S.O.R. 7 3	
			Transferred D.R.S. O.R. ×1 1	
			Hospital admitted – 3	W.M.F.
	3.9.16		O.R. 30 5	
			Evacuated C.C.S. O.R. 15 4	
			Transferred D.R.S. O.R. 9 2	
			Died at A.D.S. 1 –	
			Discharged Duty 1	

Army Form C. 2118.

WAR DIARY
or
INTELLIGENCE SUMMARY.
(Erase heading not required.)

Place	Date	Hour	Summary of Events and Information	Remarks and references to Appendices
Same	3.9.16		Capt. T. Rees. R.A.M.C. and 1 N.C.O. attended for instruction at Divisional Gas School. Lt. D.R. Taylor, R.A.M.C. returned from Overleere.	W.D.S.
	4.9.16		Hospital admitted. Sick wounded O.R. 15 nil Evacuated C.C.S. O.R. 9 nil Transferred D.R.S. O.R. 16 1 " 130 Fd Amb. O.R. 1 nil	W.D.S.

	5.9.16		Lt. D.R. Taylor, R.A.M.C. proceeded on leave.
			 Hospital admitted Officers 1 sick wounded nil
			    O.R. 24 8
			 Evacuated to C.C.S. Officers 1 nil
			    O.R. 9 5
			 Transferred D.R.S. Officers — nil
			    O.R. 6 1
			 Transferred 130 Fd Amb. O.R. 1 —
			 Discharged Duty O.R. — 1
				W.D.S.

WAR DIARY
or
INTELLIGENCE SUMMARY.

(Erase heading not required.)

Army Form C. 2118.

Place	Date	Hour	Summary of Events and Information		Remarks and references to Appendices
Same	6.9.16		Hospital Admissions		
			Officer	1	
			O.R.	12 Sick / nil Wounded	
			Evacuated to C.C.S. O.R.	6 Sick / 8 Wounded	
			Transferred to D.R.S. Officers	1 / nil	8 including one S.I. to BOES CHEPE
			O.R.	4 / 2	WBC
	7.9.16		Hospital Admissions		
			O.R.	17 / 6	
			Evacuated to C.C.S. O.R.	nil / 3	
			Transferred to D.R.S. O.R.	9 / 1	
			Died	nil / 1	
	8.9.16		Hospital Admissions		
			O.R.	10 / 15	WBC
			Evacuated to C.C.S. Officers	1 / nil	
			O.R.	17 / 7	
			Transferred to D.R.S. O.R.	11 / 2	WBC

WAR DIARY
or
INTELLIGENCE SUMMARY.

Army Form C. 2118.

Place	Date	Hour	Summary of Events and Information	Remarks and references to Appendices
Same	9.9.16		Hospital Admissions	
			Officers Sick 2 wounded nil	
			O.R. 22 nil	
			Evacuated to C.C.S. O.R. 8 "	
			Transferred to D.R.S. O.R. 5 5	
			Evacuated to Spec. Hospital BOESCHEPE O.R. 2	WBE
	10.9.16		Hospital Admitted Sick wounded	
			Officers 1 1	
			O.R. 20 "	
			Evacuated C.C.S. O.R. 8 9	
			Transferred D.R.S. 3 1	
			130th Field Amb. O.R. 1 nil	WBE

WAR DIARY
or
INTELLIGENCE SUMMARY.
(Erase heading not required.)

Army Form C. 2118.

Place	Date	Hour	Summary of Events and Information	Remarks and references to Appendices
Sama	11.9.16		Hospital. Admitted Sick Wounded	
			Officers nil 1	
			O.R. 25 8	
			Evacuated to C.C.S. Officers 2 1	
			O.R. 14 6	
			Transferred to D.R.S. O.R. 7 5	
			Transferred to 130th Field Amb. O.R. 1 nil	
			Discharged to duty O.R. 1	WRR
	12.9.16		Hospital Admitted Sick Wounded	
			Officers nil 1	
			O.R. 19 4	
			Evacuated to C.C.S. Officers 1 —	
			O.R. 11 8	
			Transferred to 130 Field Amb. O.R. — —	
			Discharged to duty O.R. 6 —	WRR

WAR DIARY
or
INTELLIGENCE SUMMARY.

Army Form C. 2118.

Place	Date	Hour	Summary of Events and Information	Remarks and references to Appendices
Same	12.9.16		Capt. L.L. HADLEY R.A.M.C. returned from leave & proceeded to take over medical charge of 13th Batt. R.W.F. Capt. T.T. REES took over charge of the A.D.S. Lt. J.G.S. MENZIE R.A.M.C. returned to main dressing station from A.D.S. W.B.E	

WAR DIARY
or
INTELLIGENCE SUMMARY.
(Erase heading not required.)

Army Form C. 2118.

Place	Date	Hour	Summary of Events and Information	Remarks and references to Appendices
Same	13.9.16		Hospital Admitted Sick Wounded	
			Officers nil 1	
			O.R. 18 17	
			Evacuated to C.C.S. Officers nil 1	
			O.R. 19 19	
			Evacuated Special Hospital Borscheke. O.R. 1 (Self Inflicted)	
			Transferred D.R.S. O.R. 8 2	
			Discharged Duty O.R. 1 nil	
			Died at A.D.S. 2	
			Capt G. HAMILTON reported for duty and taken on the strength of the Unit	4/7F
			Capt HAMILTON R.A.M.C. proceeded for duty at the A.D.S	
			Sgt KELLY returned from leave	
Same	14.9.16		Hospital Admitted Sick Wounded	
			Officers 1 1	
			O.R. 11 5	
			Evacuated C.C.S. O.R. 8 5	M7/F

Army Form C. 2118.

WAR DIARY
or
INTELLIGENCE SUMMARY.
(Erase heading not required.)

Instructions regarding War Diaries and Intelligence Summaries are contained in F. S. Regs., Part II. and the Staff Manual respectively. Title pages will be prepared in manuscript.

Place	Date	Hour	Summary of Events and Information	Remarks and references to Appendices
Same	14.9.16		Hospital Sick wounded	
			Transferred D.R.S. O.R. 8 4	
			Discharged to Duty O.R. nil 1	
	15.9.16		Hospital Admitted Sick wounded	W768
			Officers 1 4	
			O.R. 16 34	
			Evacuated C.C.S. Officers 1 5	
			O.R. 10 12	
			Transferred D.R.S. O.R. 8 2	
			Discharged to Duty O.R. 1 nil	
			Died at A.D.S. O.R. nil 1	
			Lt. J.W.RIDDEL R.A.M.C. returned to main Dressing station from A.D.S.	
			Lt. T.KELLY R.A.M.C. proceeded on temporary duty as M.O. 10th Bn. S.W.B.	
	16.9.16		Hospital admitted sick wounded	W768.
			Officer nil 1	
			O.R. 4 8	
			Evacuated C.C.S. Officer 1 2	
			O.R. 3 8	

WAR DIARY
or
INTELLIGENCE SUMMARY.
(Erase heading not required.)

Army Form C. 2118.

Place	Date	Hour	Summary of Events and Information	Remarks and references to Appendices
Somme	16.9.16		Hospital Sick Wounded Transferred to D.R.S. O.R. 6 5	J/458

	17.9.16		Hospital Admitted Sick Wounded
			      Officers 1 nil
			      O.R. 19 4
			 Evacuated C.C.S. O.R. 6 4
			 Transferred D.R.S. O.R. 7 3
				D.R.S.

	18.9.16		Hospital Admitted Sick Wounded O.R. 14 1 Evacuated C.C.S. O.R. 6 nil Transferred D.R.S. O.R. 4 3 Transferred 130th Fd Amb. O.R. 1 nil Lt. H.R. HURTER R.A.M.C. proceeded for duty to A.D.M.S. 14th Division	

	19.9.16		Hospital Admitted Sick Wounded
			      Officer 1 nil
			      O.R. 19 1
				6759

Army Form C. 2118.

WAR DIARY
or
INTELLIGENCE SUMMARY.
(Erase heading not required.)

Instructions regarding War Diaries and Intelligence Summaries are contained in F. S. Regs., Part II. and the Staff Manual respectively. Title pages will be prepared in manuscript.

Place	Date	Hour	Summary of Events and Information	Remarks and references to Appendices
Somme	19.9.16		Hospital Sick 3 Wounded nil	3.g.int
	20.9.16		Transferred to D.R.S. admitted	
			Evacuated C.C.S. O.R. 20 13	
			Transferred D.R.S. O.R. 13 9	W.F.B.
			Admitted Officers 12 2	
			O.R. 1 nil	
	21.9.16		Evacuated C.C.S. O.R. 14 1	
			Transferred to D.R.S. O.R. 5 4	
			130th F.Amb. O.R. 6 3	
			Lt. J.H. BANKES R.A.M.C. joined for duty from the 130th Field Amb. 1 nil	W.F.B.S.
			Lt. G.W. RIDDEL proceeded to OXALEARE to attend a class of instruction on Gas.	
	22.9.16		Hospital admitted Sick Wounded	
			O.R. 20 nil	

WAR DIARY
or
INTELLIGENCE SUMMARY.

(Erase heading not required.)

Army Form C. 2118.

Place	Date	Hour	Summary of Events and Information	Remarks and references to Appendices
Samer	22.9.16		Hospital admitted sick wounded	
			Evacuated C.C.S. Officers 1 nil	
			O.R. — 1	
			Transferred to D.R.S. O.R. 11 nil	
			Transferred to 130th F.Amb. O.R. 1 nil	
	23.9.16		Lt. J.H.Bankes R.A.M.C proceeded for duty to A.D.S.	W785
			Capt R. HAMILTON R.A.M.C returned for duty to the main dressing station from the A.D.S.	
			Hospital admitted sick wounded	
			Officers nil 2	
			O.R. 18 2	
			Evacuated to C.C.S. Officers nil 2	
			O.R. 5 nil	
			Transferred to D.R.S. Officers 1 nil	
			O.R. 4 nil	
			Transferred to 130th F.Amb. O.R. 1 nil	W785

Army Form C. 2118.

WAR DIARY
or
INTELLIGENCE SUMMARY.
(Erase heading not required.)

Instructions regarding War Diaries and Intelligence Summaries are contained in F. S. Regs., Part II. and the Staff Manual respectively. Title pages will be prepared in manuscript.

Place	Date	Hour	Summary of Events and Information			Remarks and references to Appendices
Same	24.9.16		Hospital	Admitted	Sick	Wounded	
				O.R.	21	1	
			Evacuated to C.C.S.	O.R.	8	2	
			Transferred to D.R.S.	O.R.	10	Nil	WT&F
			Discharged to Duty	O.R.	2	Nil	
Same	25.9.16		Lt. G.W. RIDDEL R.A.M.C returned to main dressing station from OXALAERE. for duty.				
			Hospital		Sick	Wounded	
			Admitted	Officers	2	Nil	
				O.R.	19	1	
			Evacuated to C.C.S.	Officers	1	Nil	
				O.R.	3	3	
			Transferred to D.R.S.	O.R.	6	1	WT&F
			Hospital		Sick	Wounded	
26.9.16			Admitted	Officers	2	Nil	
				O.R.	19 (1 A.S.I)	2	
			Evacuated to C.C.S.	Officers	2	Nil	
				O.R.	13	3	
			Transferred D.R.S	O.R.	11	Nil	WT&F

Army Form C. 2118.

WAR DIARY
or
INTELLIGENCE SUMMARY.
(Erase heading not required.)

Instructions regarding War Diaries and Intelligence Summaries are contained in F. S. Regs., Part II. and the Staff Manual respectively. Title pages will be prepared in manuscript.

Place	Date	Hour	Summary of Events and Information	Remarks and references to Appendices
Somme	27.9.16		Hospital Sick Wounded	
			Admitted O.R. 18 5	
			Evacuated C.C.S. O.R. 5 (1 + S.I.) 5	
			Transferred D.R.S. O.R. 10 nil	
			Discharged Duty O.R. 2 nil	
	28.9.16		Hospital Sick Wounded	W785
			Admitted Officers 2 nil	
			O.R. 49 5	
			Evacuated C.C.S. Officers 2 nil	
			O.R. 13 2	
			Transferred D.R.S. 12 3	
			Lt. G.W. Riddel R.A.M.C. proceeded on leave 29.9.16 to 13.10.16	W788
	29.9.16		Hospital Sick Wounded	
			Admitted 29 11	
			Evacuated C.C.S. 14 10	
			Transferred D.R.S. 19 1	W785

WAR DIARY
or
INTELLIGENCE SUMMARY.

(Erase heading not required.)

Army Form C. 2118.

Place	Date	Hour	Summary of Events and Information	Remarks and references to Appendices
Somme	30.9.16		Hospital Sick Wounded	
			admitted Officers 1 nil	
			" O.R. 7 nil	
			Evacuated C.C.S. Officers 1 nil	
			O.R. 10 nil	
			Transferred D.R.S. Officers 1 nil	
			O.R. 8 nil	WT3 ?

J. Stockerton Edwards
Lt. Colonel, R.A.M.C.
O.C. 129th FIELD AMBULANCE,
38 (WELSH) DIVISION.

38th Div

140/1815.

WAR DIARY.

129th Field Ambulance.

OCTOBER 1916

Original
Oct.1916

COMMITTEE FOR THE
MEDICAL HISTORY OF THE WAR
Date -9 DEC. 1919

Army Form C. 2118.

WAR DIARY
or
INTELLIGENCE SUMMARY.
(Erase heading not required.)

Instructions regarding War Diaries and Intelligence Summaries are contained in F. S. Regs., Part II. and the Staff Manual respectively. Title pages will be prepared in manuscript.

Place	Date	Hour	Summary of Events and Information	Remarks and references to Appendices
A23.C.2.9	1.10.16		Hospital Sick Wounded	
			admitted Officers nil 1	
			OR 28 8	
			Evacuated C.C.S. Officers nil 1	
			OR 15 17	10785
			Transferred D.R.S. OR 21 nil	
			Discharged to Duty Officers 1 nil	
			Capt. T. KELLY R.A.M.C. returned for duty from the 10th S.H.B.	
			Capt. T. KELLY R.A.M.C. proceeded to the A.D.S. for duty	
2.10.16			Hospital Sick Wounded	
			admitted Officers 1 nil	
			OR 16 7	
			Evacuated C.C.S. 9 5	10788
			sick wounded	
3.10.16			Hospital admitted Officers 3 nil	
			OR 13 8	
			Evacuated C.C.S. Officers 1 nil	
			OR 3 9	

Army Form C. 2118.

WAR DIARY
or
INTELLIGENCE SUMMARY.

(Erase heading not required.)

Instructions regarding War Diaries and Intelligence Summaries are contained in F. S. Regs., Part II. and the Staff Manual respectively. Title pages will be prepared in manuscript.

Place	Date	Hour	Summary of Events and Information	Remarks and references to Appendices
Somme	2.10.16		Transferred D.R.S. Sick wounded " C.R.S. 24 nil Discharged Duty Officers 1 nil O.R. nil	

	4.10.16		Capt. F.T. REES R.A.M.C. returned to duty from the A.D.S
			Capt. W.J.S. MENNIE proceeded on leave from 4.10.16 to 18.10.16
			                      Sick wounded
			Hospital Admitted Officers 2 1
			                 O.R. 34 7
			Evacuated C.C.S. O.R. 9 2
			Transferred D.R.S. O.R. 8 nil
			Discharged to duty O.R. 5 nil
			Died at A.D.S. O.R. nil 1
				WJSE

	5.10.16		Sick wounded
			Hospital
			   Admitted O.R. 26 1
			Evacuated C.C.S. Officers 1 nil
			                   O.R. 5 1
				WJSE

WAR DIARY
or
INTELLIGENCE SUMMARY.
(Erase heading not required.)

Army Form C. 2118.

Place	Date	Hour	Summary of Events and Information	Remarks and references to Appendices
Same	5.10.16		Transferred D.R.S. O.R. Sick 20 Wounded 2	WR
			" C.R.S. Officers 2 1	
	6.10.16		Hospital Sick Wounded	
			Admitted Officers nil 1	
			O.R. 22 3	
			Evacuated C.C.S. Officers 1 1	
			O.R. 11 3	
			Transferred D.R.S. O.R. 10 nil	
			" C.R.S. Officers 1 1	
			Hospital Admitted Officers nil 2	WR
			O.R. 11 1	
	7.10.16		Evacuated C.C.S. Officers nil 1	
			O.R. 7 nil	
			Transferred D.R.S. O.R. 17 1	
			Discharged to Duty O.R. 1 nil	WR

WAR DIARY
or
INTELLIGENCE SUMMARY.

(Erase heading not required.)

Army Form C. 2118.

Place	Date	Hour	Summary of Events and Information	Remarks and references to Appendices
Corps	8.10.16		Hospital Sick Wounded	
			Admitted Officers 2 nil	
			O.R. 38 9	
			Evacuated C.C.S. O.R. 17 5	
			Transferred D.R.S. 9 1	
			Discharged to Duty 3 nil	
			Died at A.D.S. nil 1	W78.
	9.10.16		Capt. C.W. NEADEN R.A.M.C. returned for Duty	
			Hospital Sick Wounded	
			Admitted O.R. 18 5	
			Evacuated C.C.S. O.R. 3 2	
			Transferred D.R.S. O.R. 20 3	
			Hospital Admitted O.R. 5 3	
			Evacuated C.C.S. Officers 3 1	
			O.R. 5 4	W78.2
	10.10.16		Transferred C.R.S. Officers 1 1	
			D.R.S. O.R. 15 nil	
			Discharged Duty O.R. 1 nil	W78.

WAR DIARY
or
INTELLIGENCE SUMMARY.

(Erase heading not required.)

Army Form C. 2118.

Place	Date	Hour	Summary of Events and Information	Remarks and references to Appendices
Somme	11.10.16		Hospital	
			Admitted O.R. Sick 30 wounded nil	
			Evacuated C.C.S. Officers 1 nil	
			O.R. 2 nil	
			Transferred D.R.S. O.R. 7 6	W.B.5
			" 130. 7⁰ Amb. O.R. 2 nil	
	12.10.16		Hospital	
			Admitted Officers nil wounded	
			O.R. 23 6	
			Evacuated C.C.S. Officers nil nil	
			O.R. 11 6	
			Transferred D.R.S. O.R. 12 1	
			Admitted Officers — —	
			O.R. 19 28	W.B.9
	13.10.16		Evacuated C.C.S. Officers nil 3	
			O.R. nil 27	
			Transferred D.R.S. Officers 2 2	
			D.R.S. O.R. 15 2	

Army Form C. 2118.

WAR DIARY
or
INTELLIGENCE SUMMARY.
(Erase heading not required.)

Instructions regarding War Diaries and Intelligence Summaries are contained in F. S. Regs., Part II. and the Staff Manual respectively. Title pages will be prepared in manuscript.

Place	Date	Hour	Summary of Events and Information	Remarks and references to Appendices
	13.10.16		S/Lt D.R. TAYLOR R.A.M.C. is struck off the strength of the Unit from 13.9.16	WSP
	14.10.16		Lt G.W. RIDDEL R.A.M.C. returned from leave. Capt R.G. HAMILTON R.A.M.C. proceeded for Temporary duty as M.O. 8th Corps Cavalry Regt.	
			Sick Wounded	
			Hospital Admitted Officers 1 2	
			O.R. 9 21	
			Evacuated C.C.S. Officers nil 1	
			O.R. 13 9	
			Transferred D.R.S. O.R. 11 4	
			Died O.R. — 1	WSP
	15.10.16		Hospital Admitted Officers 2 nil	
			O.R. 29 4	
			Evacuated C.C.S. Officers 1 nil	
			O.R. 3 5	
			Transferred D.R.S. O.R. 17 3	
			" 130th Fd Amb O.R. 1 nil	
			Discharged Duty O.R. 2 nil	

WAR DIARY
or
INTELLIGENCE SUMMARY.
(Erase heading not required.)

Army Form C. 2118.

Place	Date	Hour	Summary of Events and Information	Remarks and references to Appendices
	15.10.16		Capt. C.A. MEADEN R.A.M.C. proceeded for temporary duty as M.O. to left Group R.F.A. at B.28.a.9.2. map 28.	M78.
			Capt. R.G. ABRAHAMS. R.A.M.C. joined for duty	M78.
	16.10.16		Hospital sick wounded	
			Casualties Officers 2 nil	
			O.R. 5 8	
			Transferred C.R.S. Officers 2 nil	
			" D.R.S. O.R. 9 1	
			Evacuated C.C.S. Officers 2 nil	
			O.R. 4 3	
			Discharged Duty O.R. 2 nil	
			Died at A.D.S. O.R. nil 3	
	17.10.16		Hospital Admission Officers 2 nil	M78.
			Evacuated C.C.S. O.R. 32 2	
			Transferred D.R.S. O.R. 3 1	
			Discharged Duty O.R. 1 nil	M78.

Army Form C. 2118.

WAR DIARY
or
INTELLIGENCE SUMMARY.
(Erase heading not required.)

Instructions regarding War Diaries and Intelligence Summaries are contained in F. S. Regs., Part II. and the Staff Manual respectively. Title pages will be prepared in manuscript.

Place	Date	Hour	Summary of Events and Information			Remarks and references to Appendices
Same	18.10.16		Hospital	Sick	Wounded	
			Admitted Officers	1	nil	
			O.R.	27	1	
			Evacuated C.C.S. O.R.	5	nil	
			Transferred C.R.S. Officers	1	nil	
			hills D.R.S. O.R.	10	nil	
			Dulli 130th Field Amb OR	2	nil	
			Discharged Duty O.R.	6	nil	W.T.S.
	19.10.16		Hospital. Admitted. Officers	1	nil	
			" O.R.	28	nil	
			Evacuated C.C.S. Officers	1	nil	
			O.R.	13	2	
			Transferred D.R.S. O.R	6	1	
			Dulli 130th Field Amb. O.R.	3	nil	
			Discharged duty O.R.	1	nil	W.T.S.

WAR DIARY
or
INTELLIGENCE SUMMARY.
(Erase heading not required.)

Army Form C. 2118.

Place	Date	Hour	Summary of Events and Information	Remarks and references to Appendices
SAMMU	20.10.16		Capt. RIDDELL R.A.M.C proceeded for duty to the A.D.S. to relieve S=BANKES who returned for duty to main dressing station. Capt. J.G.S. MENNIE R.A.M.C returned from leave 19.10.16 Hospital	S=BANKES
			Sick Wounded	
			Admitted O.R 17 3	
			Evacuated C.C.S. O.R 10 nil	
			Transferred D.R.S. O.R 6 nil	
			Ditto E.R.S. Officers 1 nil	
			Discharged Duty O.R — nil	
	21.10.16		Hospital Admitted Officers nil 1	
			O.R 13 6	
			Evacuated C.C.S Officers nil 1	1788
			O.R 15 9	
			Transferred D.R.S. O.R 11 nil	
			to 130 Jo Amb O.R 1 nil	
			Discharge Duty O.R 3 nil	
			Hospital Admitted Officers nil nil	
	22.10.16		O.R 19 10	
			Evacuated C.C.S. Officers nil 2	
			O.R 6 7	
			Transferred D.R.S. Officers 18 nil	
			Discharged Duty O.R 1 nil	
			Capt J.G.S Mennie R.A.M.C proceeded to take over temporary charge of the 11th Bat. R.W.F as M.O.	W.W.F

WAR DIARY
or
INTELLIGENCE SUMMARY.

(Erase heading not required.)

Army Form C. 2118.

Place	Date	Hour	Summary of Events and Information	Remarks and references to Appendices
Cornu	23.10.16		Lt. J.H. BANKES. R.A.M.C proceeded to take over temporary medical charge of the 38th Div Engineers.	
			Capt. Rex A. HUGHES C.F. taken on the ration strength of the Unit.	
				wounded
			Hospital admitted .... Officers 3 / O.R. 18	nil / 10
			" "	
			Evacuated C.C.S. .... O.R. 5	8
			Transferred D.R.S. .... O.R. 8	nil
			Discharged Duty .... O.R. — 2	nil
24.10.16			Hospital admitted .... Officer 2 / O.R. 24	nil	W75-9
			Evacuated C.C.S. .... O.R. 8	nil
			Transferred D.R.S. .... O.R. 11	1
			Discharged Duty .... O.R. nil	nil	W79
25.10.16			Hospital admitted .... O.R. 24	nil
			Evacuated C.C.S. .... Officer 1	nil
			" " .... O.R. 2	2
			Transferred C.R.S. .... Officer 1	nil
			Ditto D.R.S. .... O.R. 13	1	W78
			Ditto 130th F. Amb. .... O.R. 3	nil
			Discharged Duty .... O.R. 3	nil

Army Form C. 2118.

WAR DIARY
or
INTELLIGENCE SUMMARY.
(Erase heading not required.)

Instructions regarding War Diaries and Intelligence Summaries are contained in F.S. Regs., Part II. and the Staff Manual respectively. Title pages will be prepared in manuscript.

Place	Date	Hour	Summary of Events and Information	Remarks and references to Appendices
Somme	26.10.16		Hospital admitted O.R. Sick 23	
			Evacuated C.C.S. O.R. 5	
			Transferred D.R.S. O.R. 4	
			" 130 & 3 Am.b. O.R. 9 wd	
			" " " O.R. 2 nil	
			Capt. J.G.S. MENNIE R.A.M.C. reported from the 115th Bat. R.W.F. Regt.	
			Capt. T. KELLY R.A.M.C. returned for duty to the main dressing station from 15 A.D.S.	W785.
	27.10.16		Hospital admitted Officers 1 Sick 25 wounded	
			Evacuated C.C.S. O.R. 5 nil	
			Transferred D.R.S. O.R. 16	
			" 130 & 3 Amb. O.R. 2 nil	
			Discharged Duty O.R. 2 nil	
	28.10.16		Hospital admitted O.R. 6 1	W788.
			Evacuated C.C.S. O.R. 16 1	
			Transferred C.R.S. Officers 9 (last)	
			" D.R.S. O.R. 27 wd	
			" 130 & 3 Amb. O.R. 2 wd	
			Discharged Duty O.R. 2 wd	W798.

Army Form C. 2118.

WAR DIARY
or
INTELLIGENCE SUMMARY.
(Erase heading not required.)

Instructions regarding War Diaries and Intelligence Summaries are contained in F. S. Regs., Part II. and the Staff Manual respectively. Title pages will be prepared in manuscript.

Place	Date	Hour	Summary of Events and Information			Remarks and references to Appendices
Same	29.10.16		Hospital admitted Officers	Sick 3	Wounded nil	
			Evacuated C.C.S. O/R.	2/6	nil	
			Transferred D.R.S. O.R.	nil	nil	
			" 130th F.Amb. O.R.	7	1	W185.
			Discharged Duty O.R.	1	nil	
			" O.R.	1	nil	
30.10.16			Hospital Admitted Officers	nil	1	
			" O.R.	22	3	
			Evacuated C.C.S. Officers	nil	1	
			" O.R.	11	2	W185.
			Transferred D.R.S. O.R.	11	nil	
			Discharged Duty O.R.	1	nil	
31.10.16			Hospital Admitted Officers	1	nil	
			" O.R.	20	8	
			Evacuated C.C.S. Officers	nil	nil	
			" O.R.	4	8	
			Transferred to D.R.S. O.R.	8	nil	W185.

W. Bickerton Edwards
Lt. Colonel, R.A.M.C.
O.C. 129th FIELD AMBULANCE,
(WELSH) DIVISION,

Original copy.
140/262
Vol 9

38th Divn

WAR DIARY.

129th Field Ambulance

November 1916

Received 2nd Nov

COMMITTEE FOR THE
MEDICAL HISTORY OF THE WAR.
Date — 3 JAN. 1917

Army Form C. 2118.

WAR DIARY
or
INTELLIGENCE SUMMARY.
(Erase heading not required.)

Instructions regarding War Diaries and Intelligence Summaries are contained in F. S. Regs., Part II. and the Staff Manual respectively. Title pages will be prepared in manuscript.

Place	Date	Hour	Summary of Events and Information	Remarks and references to Appendices

A.23.C.2.9 Map Sheet 28	1.11.16		Hospital. Remaining Officers Sick Wounded
			                               O.R. 4 nil
			                                      77 4	

	2.11.16		Capt. C.A. MEADEN returned to Duty
			Capt. R.G. ABRAHAMS. R.A.M.C. proceeded to Hd 10th Bat West Rt Surrey for duty
			Hospital. Remaining Officers Sick Wounded
			                                    O.R. 3 nil
			                                      80 5
				WBS
				
				WBC

	3.11.16		Three cases from among personnel of this 5p.[Amb], convalescent after P.U.O show loss of knee jerk. Capt. R.G. ABRAHAMS. Struck off the Strength of the unit. Inspected and reported upon the A.D.S. at Essex & Sussex Farms. Six rats taken from ATLAS TRENCH for examination at Bacteriological 20.6.10. C.C.S
			Hospital. Remaining Officers Sick Wounded
			                                  O.R. 4 nil
			                                    80 3
				WBS

	4.11.16		Ditto Ditto Officers Sick Wounded
			                                  O.R. 4 nil
			                                    90 3
				WTSS

	5.11.16		A.D.M.S. visited Dressing Station. Called attention of A.D.M.S. & O.C. Sanitary Section 15 observed of knee jerks in certain convalescents after P.U.O. 4 long & 1 small concrete Dugouts taken over from 4th L.F.A. Bat. 12 F. for A.D.S. on Canal Bank.
			Hospital. Remaining Officers Sick Wounded
			                                  O.R. 5 1
			                                    102 3
				WTS

Army Form C. 2118.

WAR DIARY
or
INTELLIGENCE SUMMARY.
(Erase heading not required.)

Place	Date	Hour	Summary of Events and Information	Remarks and references to Appendices
Somme	6.11.16		Hospital Remaining. Officers O.R. Sick 2 Wounded 1 / 90 3	
	7.11.16		Lt. J.H. BANKES. R.A.M.C. returned to main Dressing station for Duty.	W.75.B.
			Hospital Remaining Officers 3 Sick Wounded O.R. 71 1	
			A.D.M.S. Inspected the Hospital. Lt. J.H. BANKES. R.A.M.C. proceeded for duty on the central bank under O.C. Sanitary Sec. Capt. C.A. MEADEN R.A.M.C. proceeded for duty at the A.D.S. Capt. G.W. RIDDEL returned for duty to the main dressing station from the A.D.S.	W.75.E.
	8.11.16		Hospital remaining Officers 3 Sick Wounded O.R. 58 nil	
			Accompanied the A.D.M.S. on an inspection of the A.D.S	W.75.C.
	9.11.16		Hospital Remaining Officers 1 Wounded O.R. 52 me 1	
			Capt. J.G.S. MENNIE R.A.M.C. returned to headquarters from the A.D.S. & was admitted to Hospital suffering from P.U.O. Capt. T. KELLY proceed for duty to the A.D.S. Capt. F.T. REES R.A.M.C. proceed the A.D.S. & aid book with the D.A.D.M.S. Capt. F.T. REES R.A.M.C. visited the A.D.S. & aid book with the D.A.D.M.S.	

WAR DIARY
or
INTELLIGENCE SUMMARY.
(Erase heading not required.)

Army Form C. 2118.

Place	Date	Hour	Summary of Events and Information	Remarks and references to Appendices
Sarn	9.11.16		D.D.M.S. visited main Dressing Station.	W.T.P.?
	10.11.16		Hospital. Remaining Officers 2, O.R. 51, sick	W.T.P.?
	11.11.16		Hospital Remaining Officers 3, O.R. 61, sick 2	
			Personnel at main dressing station are still busy engaged in Hospital work, erection of new Huts & Dug outs, Construction of additional structures, excavation of new drainage system. At the A.D.S. in addition to routine work repairing of Dug outs, completing new Concrete Dug outs is being carried out, fitting out as Hospital with trestles, tables &c. wounded nil	W.T.P.?
	12.11.16		Hospital. Remaining Officers 2, O.R. 52, sick 3	
			Capt. F.T. Rees R.A.M.C. visited A.D.S. to arrange Billets & for R.A.M.C. labour party attached to R.E.'s.	W.T.P.?
	13.11.16		New Steel Shelter obtained from R.E.'s for our men at La Belle Alliance side door. Capt. HAMILTON R.A.M.C. reported for duty from Turnstiles Co.	

Army Form C. 2118.

WAR DIARY
or
INTELLIGENCE SUMMARY.
(Erase heading not required.)

Instructions regarding War Diaries and Intelligence Summaries are contained in F. S. Regs., Part II. and the Staff Manual respectively. Title pages will be prepared in manuscript.

Place	Date	Hour	Summary of Events and Information	Remarks and references to Appendices
Same	13.11.16		Hospital. Remaining Officers 3 Sick, nil wounded	
			O.R. 57 3	
	14.11.16		6 of 1st convalescent. P.U.O patients in 5b isolated for Knee Jerk on or after 5th day of disease in 12. It was about 15. a o/o of 21 t WTBP	WTBP
			Hospital. Remaining Officers 3 Sick nil wounded	
			O.R. 58 3	
	15.11.16		Capt HAMILTON R.A.M.C. proceeded for temporary duty as M.O. 1st S.W.B. A.D.M.S. visited Hospital + Camp. Isolation area, wards &c. At main dressing station completed	MTK
			Hospital. Remaining Officers 2 Sick wounded	
			O.R. 67 1 nil	
	16.11.16		Hospital. Remaining Officers 2 Sick nil wounded	MTK
			O.R. 72 1	
	17.11.16		Hospital. Remaining Officers 2 Sick nil wounded	
			O.R. 60	

Army Form C. 2118.

WAR DIARY
or
INTELLIGENCE SUMMARY.
(Erase heading not required.)

Place	Date	Hour	Summary of Events and Information	Remarks and references to Appendices
Camp	18/11/16		Hospital Remaining Officers $\frac{Sick}{OR}$ $\frac{1}{59}$ Wounded nil 3	Sunt J Tavernier Res
	19/11/16		Lieut. Colonel W B EDWARDS proceeded on leave (18th - 28th Nov) Capt F.T. REES took over Temporary charge. 2 German Prisoners admitted wounded taken in raid on Night 17th-18th one of whom died in hospital same day. Hospital Remaining Officers $\frac{Sick}{OR}$ $\frac{4}{48}$ Wounded nil 2	99R.
	20/11/16		German prisoner buried at FERME OLIVIER. B.13.f.5.3 (Sheet 28) Hospital Remaining Officers $\frac{Sick}{OR}$ $\frac{4}{56}$ Wounded nil 2	99R.
	21/11/16		Remaining German Prisoner evacuated to No 46 CCS Accompanied by Colonel J. DAVIES O/C 130th Field Ambulance & inspected the ADS. Hospital Remaining Officers $\frac{Sick}{OR}$ $\frac{5}{56}$ Wounded nil 2	99R.

WAR DIARY
or
INTELLIGENCE SUMMARY.

(Erase heading not required.)

Army Form C. 2118.

Place	Date	Hour	Summary of Events and Information	Remarks and references to Appendices
Same	Same		R.A.M.C. LIEUT. J.H. BANKS joined on Canal Bank by Capt. J.E. DAVIES R.A.M.C. MO I/c 38th Div R.Es and proceeded to Divisional H.Qrs to attend to small unit in that neighbourhood.	O.R.
	22/11/16		A.D.M.S. visited main dressing station Sick Wounded Officers 2 — O.R. 59 2 The D.M.S. 2nd Army, accompanied by A.D.M.S. inspected the hospital and expressed himself as being well pleased with the work that was being done, and the structural improvements that had been/were being carried out on the subs Hospital Remaining Sick Wounded Officers 2 1 O.R. 62 2	O.R.
	23/11/16		Hospital Remaining Sick Wounded Officers 2 1 O.R. 74 4	O.R.
	24/11/16		A.D.M.S. visited Main Dressing Station. Normal accommodation of Hospital full. All cases arriving during night	O.R.

WAR DIARY
or
INTELLIGENCE SUMMARY.

(Erase heading not required.)

Army Form C. 2118.

Place	Date	Hour	Summary of Events and Information	Remarks and references to Appendices
Same	Same		24th-25th WERS sent on to 131st Field Ambulance at A 28 a 3.7	72h
			Sick Wounded	
	25/11/16		Hospital Remaining Officers — —	
			OR 64 —	72R
	26/11/16		Hospital Remaining Officers 1 —	
			OR 64 2	80R
	27/11/16		Hospital Remaining Officers 1 —	
			OR 62 2	89R
			Capt KELLY RAMC Proceeded for temporary duty as MO/C 14th WOR Regt in relief of Capt A R WILLIAMS RAMC. Capt J.G.S. MENNIE RAMC and Capt G W RIDDEL RAMC relieved Capt CAMERON RAMC and Capt T KELLY RAMC at the ADS.	
			Sick Wounded	
	28/11/16		Hospital Remaining Officers 1 —	
			OR 60 2	90R
			Proceeded to CANAL BANK to arrange billets for RAMC working party and inspected to ADS	93R

WAR DIARY
or
INTELLIGENCE SUMMARY.

Army Form C. 2118.

Place	Date	Hour	Summary of Events and Information	Remarks and references to Appendices
Same	29/11/16		Hospital Remaining Officers - OR 61 Sick 1 Wounded - 2 A.D.M.S. intimated illness of Lieut Col W.B EDWARDS RAMC while on leave	M.R
Same	30/11/16		LIEUT & QM J VARLEY RAMC proceeded on leave (30th - 10/12/16) CAPTAIN A. HUGHES, C.F. proceeded to England and was struck off the strength of unit. Hospital Remaining Officers 1 OR 70 Sick - 2	M.R

G Dawson Rees Capt RAMC
O.i/c 129th Field Ambulance
38th (Welsh) Division

32 M.D.
14 Copies

Vol 10

War Diary
129th Field Ambulance
December 1916

Secret.
Dec 1916

Original Copy

COMMITTEE FOR THE
MEDICAL HISTORY OF THE WAR
Date 31 JAN. 1917

WAR DIARY
or
INTELLIGENCE SUMMARY.

Army Form C. 2118.

Place	Date	Hour	Summary of Events and Information	Remarks and references to Appendices
A 23 c 2.9	1/7/16		Hospital Remaining Officers 3 / O.R. 77	
	2/7/16		A Private in the French Army admitted to Hospital wounded. Lieut F.H. BANKES RAMC rejoined for duty from Divisional Hdqrs. Hospital Remaining Officers 1 wounded / O.R. 70 5.	JR
	3/7/16		Lt.Colonel J.E.H. DAVIES RAMC & Lt.Col ELLIS RAMC O/c 46 C.C.S. called & were shown new Hospital & Camp. Hospital Remaining Officers 3 wounded 1 / O.R. 73 1.	JR
	4/7/16		Capt O.A. MEADON RAMC proceeded for temporary duty with 16th R.W.F. in relief of Lieut AOLT RAMC. Hospital Remaining Officers 4 wounded / O.R. 76 2	JR
			Capt A.G.S. RICHARDS RAMC 2/1 West Lancs Fld Ambce and Lieut C.W. ANDERSON RAMC 133 Field Ambce joined for temporary duty	JR

WAR DIARY
or
INTELLIGENCE SUMMARY.

Army Form C. 2118.

Place	Date	Hour	Summary of Events and Information	Remarks and references to Appendices
Same	5/12/16		Hospital Remaining Officers O.R. Sick 4 82 Wounded - 2	J.R.
	6/12/16		Capt J.G.S. MENNIE. R.A.M.C. proceeded for temporary duty with 13th R.W.F. Lieut C.M. ANDERSON. R.A.M.C. proceeded to A.D.S. Hospital Remaining Officers. O.R. Sick 4 80 Wounded - 3	J.R.
	7/12/16		D.A.D.M.S. called Hospital Remaining Officers O.R. Sick 2 77 Wounded - 3	J.R.
	8.12.16		Lieut Col W.B. EDWARDS R.A.M.C. returned from leave Hospital Remaining Officers Sick wounded O.R. 1 2 61	5TK.i.
			Capt A.G.S. RICHARDS R.A.M.C. rejoined 2nd/1 West Lanc.s Field Amb. Lt. C.M. ANDERSON R.A.M.C. returned to main dressing station from H.Q. S.O.S. Hospital. Remaining Officers 3 wounded O.R. 6 60	W/782
	9.12.16		Lt. C.M. ANDERSON & A.M.C. rejoined 133 Field Amb. Capt. G.M. EADEN R.A.M.C. returned for duty from 1/10-19.W.F.	W/785

WAR DIARY
or
INTELLIGENCE SUMMARY.

(Erase heading not required.)

Army Form C. 2118.

Place	Date	Hour	Summary of Events and Information	Remarks and references to Appendices
Same	10.12.16		Hospital Remaining Officers Sick 2 Wounded nil O.R. 72 nil	
	11.12.16		Capt. J.G.S. MENNIE. R.A.M.C. reported for duty at the A.D.S. from No 13th Bat T.N.Y. Capt. F. TREES R.A.M.C. proceeded on leave from 15.12.16 to 21st Dec. WBS Hospital Remaining Officers sick wounded nil O.R. 68 nil	
			2/Lt D. J. YARLEY returned from leave Capt. G.W. RIDDEL R.A.M.C with 17 O.R returned from the A.D.S. Essex Farm Bocq 21.22 Two h.co's & 12 other ranks took over dairy farm A.D.S from a party of 131 coy R.Am. WBS Hospital Remaining officers sick wounded 4 O.R. 74 nil 4	
	12.12.16		An advance party consisting of Capt. G.W. RIDDEL R.am.c and 1 n.c.o & 4 other men proceeded to WATOU to take over sqdn at (Sheet 27) K4B86 An advance party of two officers & 40 n.c.o's & men arrived & take over the advanced dressing stations at Essex & Sussex Farms. Capt J.G.S. MENNIES. R.A.M.C. returned to the main dressing station with the remainder of our personnel from the advanced dressing stations (Essex & Sussex Farms)	WBS

WAR DIARY or INTELLIGENCE SUMMARY.

Army Form C. 2118.

Place	Date	Hour	Summary of Events and Information	Remarks and references to Appendices
Somme	13.12.16		Hospitals. Remaining. Officers 3 Sick 2 O.R. 64 Wounded nil 3	W.T.B.E
WATOU K.43.8.6 Sheet 27.	14.12.16		The Makeshift Main Dressing Station at A.23.c.2.9. (Sheet 28) handed over to the 134 Field Ambulance at 12 noon and the Unit marched to Field Amb site at WATOU. Capt. GODFREY BATEMAN R.A.M.C. joined for duty. Hospital. Remaining. Officers 0 Sick 2 O.R. 64 Officer 0 Wounded nil 3	W.T.B.E
	15.12.16		Hospital Remaining. Officers 0 R 31 Wounded nil 1	W.T.B.E
	16.12.16		Capt. James WALKER MacDONALD R.A.M.C joined for duty. Hospital. Remaining. Officers 0 R 19 Sick Wounded nil nil	W.T.B.E
			Lt. J.H.BARKES R.A.M.C granted leave 16.12.16 to 26.12.16 Capt. C.A. MEADEN. R.A.M.C. Proceed to take over temporary charge of 122 R.F.A. Capt. HAMILTON R.A.M.C returned from 10th S.W.B as A.D.M.S inspected the Ambulance	W.T.B.E

Army Form C. 2118.

WAR DIARY
or
INTELLIGENCE SUMMARY.

(Erase heading not required.)

Place	Date	Hour	Summary of Events and Information	Remarks and references to Appendices
Somme	17.12.16		Hospital. Remaining. O.R. sick 23 wounded nil	WT8E
	18.12.16		Capt. J. BATEMAN, R.A.M.C. proceeded to take charge of the 15th Welch Regt. (Temporarily) Hospital Remaining. O.R. 28 sick wounded nil	WT8E
	19.12.16		Hospital. Remaining. O.R. 20 sick A/D.M.S. visited the Ambulance.	WT8E
	20.12.16		Hospital. Remaining. O.R. 23 sick D.D.M.S. inspected the Ambulance wounded nil	WT8E
	21.12.16		Hospital. Remaining. O.R. 18 sick wounded nil	WT8E
	22.12.16		Capt J.W. MacDONALD. R.A.M.C. proceeded to take over temporary charge of 15th Bat. Welch Regt. Hospital. Remaining. O.R. 12 sick wounded nil	WT8E
	23.12.16		Capt. F.TAVINOR REES.R.A.M.C. returned from leave Hospital. Remaining. O.R. 13 sick wounded nil	WT8E
	24.12.16		Capt. Bateman, R.A.M.C. returned from temporary duty with 15th Bat. Welch Regt. Hospital. Remaining. O.R. 9 sick wounded	WT8E

WAR DIARY
or
INTELLIGENCE SUMMARY.

Army Form C. 2118.

Place	Date	Hour	Summary of Events and Information	Remarks and references to Appendices
Suvla	25.12.16		Hospital. Remaining Sick O.R. 14 wounded	W732
	26.12.16		" O.R. 15	W788
	27.12.16		" O.R. 10 sick	W789
	28.12.16		Lt. J.H. BANKES. R.A.M.C. returned from leave. O.R. 9	
			Hospital. Remaining sick	
			Capt Hamilton. R.A.M.C. granted leave from 28.12.16 to 7.1.17	W933
	29.12.16		Hospital. Remaining O.R. 9 sick wounded	W953
			Capt. BATEMAN. R.A.M.C. proceeded for duty as M.O. to Reinforcements to Camp at H. Camp.	W953
	30.12.16		Hospital. Remaining O.R. 11 sick nil wounded	
	31.12.16		Hospital. Remaining O.R. 15 nil	W736

T.W.Belgrave Edwards
Lt. Colonel R.A.M.C.
O.C. 129th FIELD AMBULANCE,
ENGLISH DIVISION

Original Copy

38 Pages

WAR DIARY

129th Field Ambulance

January 1917

COMMITTEE FOR THE
MEDICAL HISTORY OF THE WAR
Date 13 MAR 1917

Army Form C. 2118.

WAR DIARY
or
INTELLIGENCE SUMMARY.
(Erase heading not required.)

Instructions regarding War Diaries and Intelligence Summaries are contained in F. S. Regs., Part II. and the Staff Manual respectively. Title pages will be prepared in manuscript.

125TH FIELD AMBULANCE R.A.M.C.

Place	Date	Hour	Summary of Events and Information	Remarks and references to Appendices
MATOU N4B86 Sheet 27	1.1.17		Hospital Remaining O.R. 20 Sick	
	2.1.17		Detachment of 123 Fd Amb took over A.D.S. at LARRY FARM. Lt BANKES proceeded on temporary duty as M.O. i/c 122 R.F.A.	W.B.T.
			Hospital Remaining O.R. Sick 29	W.B.T.
	3.1.17		Capt MEADEN. R.A.M.C. granted leave from 2/1/17 to 12/1/17	W.B.T.
			Hospital Remaining O.R. Sick 25	W.B.T.
	4.1.17		" " " 18	W.B.T.
	5.1.17		" " " 19	W.B.T.
	6.1.17		" " " 22	W.B.T.
			Capt MENNIE. R.A.M.C. proceeded to take over temporary medical charge 14th Bn. Welch Regt.	W.B.T.
	7.1.17		Hospital Remaining O.R. Sick 21	W.B.T.
	8.1.17		" " " 18	
			Capt MacDONALD R.A.M.C. proceeded to attend course of sanitation at HAZEBROUCK.	W.B.T.
	9.1.17		Hospital Remaining O.R. Sick 20	W.B.T.

WAR DIARY
or
INTELLIGENCE SUMMARY.

(Erase heading not required.)

Army Form C. 2118.

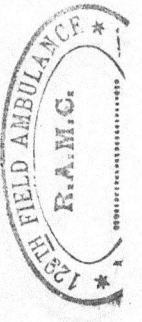

Place	Date	Hour	Summary of Events and Information	Remarks and references to Appendices
Same	10.11.17		Hospital Remaining O.R. Sick 18	
			1 N.C.O. + 3 men proceeded for duty at Water Tanks COUTHOVE	WWT
			6 men " " " " LAUNDRY "	WWT
			5 " " " " Drying Rooms POPERINGHE	WWT
	11.11.17		Hospital Remaining O.R. Sick 15	
	12.11.17		" " " 23	
	13.11.17		" " " 19	
			Advance party of 1 N.C.O. + 4 men proceeded to PROVEN	
			Lt. FRANKIES R.A.M.C. 1 N.C.O. + 19 men attached temporarily to 130th Ft. Amb	
			proceed to A.D.S. Essex Farm Canal Bank, for duty.	
			Capt. Mac'DONALD R.A.M.C. returned from Sanitary course at HAZEBROUCK. WWT	
Proven	14.11.17		Hospital Remaining O.R. Sick 23	
Fy 33 Sheet 27			Capt RIDDEL R.A.M.C. & Capt Mac'DONALD R.A.M.C. with advance party of 4 NCO's	
			and 12 men left WATOU at 6.45 P.M. to take over Ambulance site & D.R.S.	
			at Proven from the 132nd Field Amb. Main party left Watou at 10 A.M. after	
			handing over that site to 1/3 1st West LANCASHIRE Field Amb.	

Army Form C. 2118.

WAR DIARY
or
INTELLIGENCE SUMMARY.
(Erase heading not required.)

Instructions regarding War Diaries and Intelligence Summaries are contained in F. S. Regs., Part II. and the Staff Manual respectively. Title pages will be prepared in manuscript.

[Stamp: 129TH FIELD AMBULANCE R.A.M.C.]

Place	Date	Hour	Summary of Events and Information			Remarks and references to Appendices
				sick	wounded	
Same	14.1.17		Patients taken over at D.R.S from the 132nd Field Amb. O.R.	119	1	W85.
			A & D book of Divisional D.R.S. handed over to us by 131st Field Amb showed			
			28 remaining at A.R.S. 35 patients.			
	15.1.17		Hospital - Patients taken over from the 132nd Field Amb. 28.		wounded	W85.
				sick	1	
			Hospital. Remaining. D.R.S. O.R.	154	nil	
			" " Field Amb.	63		
	16.1.17		Hospital. Remaining. D.R.S. O.R.	135	1	W85.
			" " Field Amb.	35	nil	
	17.1.17		" " D.R.S. -	96	1	W85
			" " Field Amb Officers	1	nil	
			O.R.	36	nil	
	18.1.17		A.D.M.S. 38th "Welsh" Division inspected Hospital & D.R.S.			
			Hospital. Remaining. D.R.S. O.R.	59	1	
			Field Amb. Officers	1	nil	
			O.R.	37	nil	
			Capt J.W. MacDONALD. R.A.M.C proceeded for duty as temporary M.O.			W85.
			119 Brigade. R.F.A.			

Army Form C. 2118.

WAR DIARY
or
INTELLIGENCE SUMMARY.
(Erase heading not required.)

Instructions regarding War Diaries and Intelligence Summaries are contained in F. S. Regs., Part II. and the Staff Manual respectively. Title pages will be prepared in manuscript.

Place	Date	Hour	Summary of Events and Information	Remarks and references to Appendices
Somme	19.1.17		Hospital. Remaining D.R.S. O.R. Sick 71 wounded 1 " " Field Amb. " 40 " nil	W.D.S.
	20.1.17		Corps Commander 8th Corps. visited the Hospital & D.R.S. Hospital. Remaining D.R.S. O.R. sick 74 wounded 1 " " Field Amb. " 41 " nil	W.D.S.
	21.1.17		" " D.R.S. " 100 " 1 " " Field Amb. " 41 " nil	W.D.S.
	22.1.17		" " D.R.S. " 110 " 1 " " Field Amb. " 52 " - By order of A.D.M.S. 38th "Welsh" Div. Emergency bearer party of four Bec equipped so as to be available for immediate duty if required. Hospital. Remaining D.R.S. O.R. sick 96 wounded 1 " " Field Amb. " 35 " nil	W.D.S.
	23.1.17		Patients admitted to D.R.S. are given clean underclothing & baths. Uniforms, boots &c are cleaned & kits attended to. Patients during their stay are given Physical Exercises, route marches &c where required massage.	

WAR DIARY or INTELLIGENCE SUMMARY.

Army Form C. 2118.

128TH FIELD AMBULANCE R.A.M.C.

Place	Date	Hour	Summary of Events and Information	Remarks and references to Appendices
Senne	23.1.17		Capt MacDONALD. R.A.M.C. returned for Duty from Temporary duty with the 119th Brigade, R.F.A.	
			Sick Wounded	
	24.1.17		Hospital. Remaining. D.R.S. O.R. 90 1	WRS
			Field Amb Hospital 40 nil	
	25.1.17		Lt J.T. O'BOYLE. R.A.M.C. Joined for duty	WRS
			Hospital. Remaining. D.R.S. O.R. 97 2	
			F. Amb Hospital 42 "	
	26.1.17		D.R.S. O.R. 117 4	WRS
			Hospital 42 nil	WRS
	27.1.17		A.D.M.S. 38th "Welsh" Division. Inspected Hospital, D.R.S + Site.	
			Hospital Remaining. D.R.S. O.R. Sick Wounded	
			98 5	
			F.A. Hospital 36 nil	
			D.D.M.S. 8th Corps inspected D.R.S. Hospital + Site.	
			Attended conference of O.C's at A.D.M.S. office Sick Wounded	
	28.1.17		Hospital. Remaining. D.R.S. O.R. 87 5	WRS
			F° Amb. Hospital 33 nil	

WAR DIARY
or
INTELLIGENCE SUMMARY.

Army Form C. 2118.

Instructions regarding War Diaries and Intelligence Summaries are contained in F. S. Regs., Part II. and the Staff Manual respectively. Title pages will be prepared in manuscript.

(Erase heading not required.)

Place	Date	Hour	Summary of Events and Information	Remarks and references to Appendices
Same	28.1.17		Capt J.W. MacDonald R.A.M.C. proceeded for temporary duty as M.O. 10th Bn S.W.B.	WBS
				Wounded
	29.1.17		Remaining. D.R.S. O.R. Sick 89 4	WBS
			Hospital. F° Amb. Hospital 33 nil	
	30.1.17		Lt. J.T. O'Boyle R.A.M.C. proceeded for a five days course of instruction in Sanitation at HAZEBROUCK.	WBS
			Sick Wounded	
			Remaining. D.R.S. O.R. 101 4	WBS
			Hospital. F° Amb. Hospital 25 3	
	31.1.17		" D.R.S. " 108 nil	WBS
			F° Amb. Hospital 22 4	

W. Webster Edwards
Lt. Colonel R.A.M.C.
O.C. 129th FIELD AMBULANCE,
(WELSH) DIVISION.

War Diary

129th Field Ambulance

February 1917

Army Vol 12

Original Copy.

COMMITTEE FOR THE
MEDICAL HISTORY OF THE WAR
Date 4 APR 1917

Army Form C. 2118.

WAR DIARY
or
INTELLIGENCE SUMMARY.
(Erase heading not required.)

Instructions regarding War Diaries and Intelligence Summaries are contained in F. S. Regs., Part II. and the Staff Manual respectively. Title pages will be prepared in manuscript.

Place	Date	Hour	Summary of Events and Information	Remarks and references to Appendices

Proven Sh. 3.3. 27.	1.2.17		Remaining D.R.S. O.R. 85 Sick Wounded
			              Hospital " 32 16
			                                        Nil	

			Capt. KELLY. R.A.M.C. returned from leave and rejoined his Unit on 31.1.17 Capt. HAMILTON. R.A.M.C. rejoined from leave 31.1.17 & proceeded for duty with 16th Welch Regt. 1.2.17.	WTB3

	2.2.17		Remaining D.R.S. O.R. 88 Sick Wounded
			              Hospital " 32 6
			                                        Nil
				WTB3

	3.2.17		" D.R.S. 90 " 6 Hospital 33 0	
			Lt. J.T. O'BOYLE. R.A.M.C. returned from Sanitary course at HAZEBROUCK. Capt. MacDONALD. R.A.M.C. rejoined from temporary duty with the 10th Regt. S.W.B.	WTB3
			Lt. J.T.O'BOYLE. R.A.M.C. proceeded for duty as M.O. in charge of H.Q. 16th Welch Regt. A.D.M.S. visited the Hospital and addressed the Unit. Capt. MENNIE. R.A.M.C. returned to this station from the 16th Welch Regt. & proceeded	

	4.2.17		on leave 4.2.17 to 17.2.17.
			Remaining D.R.S. O.R. Sick Wounded
			             Hospital " 104 5
			                                  30
				WR2

WAR DIARY or INTELLIGENCE SUMMARY

Army Form C. 2118.

Place	Date	Hour	Summary of Events and Information	Remarks and references to Appendices
Somme	5.2.17		Remaining D.R.S. O.R. Sick Wounded	
			" Hospital 95 8	
			24 nil	
	6.2.17		A.D.M.S. (Colgill A.M.S.) inspected the Ambulance. Bomb dropped by enemy aeroplane near D.R.S. no R.A.M.C. casualties. 5 deaths & 7 wounded of other formations.	W.P.R.
			Capt. T. KELLY R.A.M.C. proceeded to 14th R.W.F. for temporary duty.	
			Remaining D.R.S. O.R. Sick	
			" Hospital 84	
			29	
	7.2.17		Capt. T. KELLY R.A.M.C. returned from the 14th Regt. R.W.F.	W.P.R.
			Remaining D.R.S. O.R. Sick Wounded	
			" Hospital 90 8	
			35 nil	
	8.2.17		D.R.S. O.R. 85 9	
			" Hospital 35 1	
	9.2.17		Capt. J.W. MacDONALD proceeded to HQ 130th Fd Amb. for Temporary Duty	W.P.R.
			A.D.M.S. visited site & models P.B. near. Lt. J.H. BANKES R.A.M.C.	
			returned from HQ 130th Field Amb.	
			Remaining D.R.S. O.R. Sick Wounded	
			" Hospital 100 13	
			35 1	W.P.R.

Instructions regarding War Diaries and Intelligence Summaries are contained in F. S. Regs., Part II. and the Staff Manual respectively. Title pages will be prepared in manuscript.

WAR DIARY
or
INTELLIGENCE SUMMARY.
(Erase heading not required.)

Army Form C. 2118.

Place	Date	Hour	Summary of Events and Information			Remarks and references to Appendices
Same	10.2.17		Remaining	O.R.	Sick	
			D.R.S.		84	
			Hospital		25	
						Wounded
	11.2.17		"	O.R.	95	10 W.S.
			D.R.S.			nil
			Hospital		34	
	12.2.17		"	"	112	9 W.S.
			D.R.S.		45	nil
			Hospital			
	13.2.17		"	"	108	8 W.S.
			D.R.S.		46	"
			Hospital			
	14.2.17		"	"	85	3 W.S.
			D.R.S.		4	nil
			Hospital			
			Conference O.C's Field Amb at A.D.M.S's office			4 W.S.?
						nil
	15.2.17		Remaining	O.R.	Sick	Wounded
			D.R.S.		105	3
			Hospital		38	1 W.S.

WAR DIARY
or
INTELLIGENCE SUMMARY.
(Erase heading not required.)

Army Form C. 2118.

Instructions regarding War Diaries and Intelligence Summaries are contained in F. S. Regs., Part II. and the Staff Manual respectively. Title pages will be prepared in manuscript.

Place	Date	Hour	Summary of Events and Information	Remarks and references to Appendices
Same	16.2.17		Brig. Gen. Atkinson, D.A.Q.M.G. VIII Corps Inspected Hospital + D.R.S.	
			Remaining: sick / wounded	
			D.R.S. O.R. 95 —	
			Hospital " 39 5	
	17.2.17		D.R.S. " 112 nil	WD38.
			Hospital " 42 5	
	18.2.17		D.R.S. " 107 1	WD38.
			Hospital " 42 1	
	19.2.17		D.R.S. " 131 9	WD38.
			Hospital " 39 1	
			Lt. J.H.BANKES, R.A.M.C. proceeded to HAZEBROUCK to attend a five day Course of Sanitation.	
	20.2.17		D.D.M.S. VIII Corps inspected Field Ambulance + D.R.S.	WD38.
			Remaining: sick / wounded	
			D.R.S. O.R. 104 6	
			Hospital " 41 —	
	21.2.17		D.R.S. " 112 1	WD38.
			Hospital " 38 —	
			A.D.M.S. inspected Field Amb + D.R.S. Conference O.C's Field Amb's at A.D.M.S's office.	WD38?

WAR DIARY
or
INTELLIGENCE SUMMARY.

Army Form C. 2118.

Place	Date	Hour	Summary of Events and Information			Remarks and references to Appendices
				Sick	Wounded	
Somme	22.2.17		Remaining D.R.S. O.R.	121	6	
			" Hospital	31	-	W78.2
	23.2.17		" D.R.S. "	93	6	
			" Hospital	42	1	W78.2
	24.2.17		" D.R.S "	93	7	
			" Hospital	44	1	W78.2
	25.2.17		" D.R.S "	96	5	
			" Hospital	38	1	W78.2
	26.2.17		2/Lt J.H.Bankes, R.A.M.C. proceed for temp duty as M.O. to Division of R.E. H.Q.s			
			10 - O.Rs returned for duty from the 130th St John's Field Amb			
			Remaining - D.R.S. O.R	89	4	
			" Hospital "	38	1	M7.93
	27.2.17		" D.R.S. "	99	5	
			" Hospital "	37	1	
	28.2.17		1 N.C.O. & 7 O.R. returned for duty from N.C. 130th "St John's" Field Amb			W78.2
			Remaining. D.R.S. O.R	84	6	
			" Hospital "	34	1	W78.2

L. Richohn Edwards
Lt. Colonel, R.A.M.C.
O.C. 129th FIELD AMBULANCE
(WELSH) DIV.

Confidential

3rd C.O. Vol /3
140/204 2

War Diary
129th Field Ambulance
March 1917

COMMITTEE FOR THE
MEDICAL HISTORY OF THE WAR
11 MAY 1917

Original Copy.

WAR DIARY or INTELLIGENCE SUMMARY

Army Form C. 2118.

Place	Date	Hour	Summary of Events and Information	Remarks and references to Appendices
Proven Fj 6.33 Sheet 27.	1.3.17		Remaining O.R. Hospital Sick 32 Wounded nil	
			" D.R.S. 83 6	M/S. Edwards
	2.3.17		Capt. J.W. MacDonald. R.A.M.C. returned from 130th Field Amb. for duty. Sick Wounded	
			Remaining O.R. Hospital 29 nil	
			" D.R.S. 82 6	WT8P
	3.3.17		Capt. J.Q.S. Mennie. R.A.M.C. reported from leave.	
			Remaining O.R. Hospital 31 nil	
			" D.R.S. 80 5	
			Capt. T. Kelly R.A.M.C. returned from Temp. duty with 13. R.W.F.	
			Capt. J.T. O'Boyle R.A.M.C. returned from Temp. duty with 14th Welch Regt.	
			Capt. J.Q.S. Mennie R.A.M.C. proceed to Traume medical Change 15th Welch Regt. WT8P	
	4.3.17		Remaining O.R. Hospital 32 wounded nil	
			" D.R.S. 88 4	WT8P
			Capt. Kelly. T. R.A.M.C. proceed for Temp. duty as M.O. 19th Welch Regt.	
	5.3.17		Remaining O.R. Hospital 26 wounded nil	
			" D.R.S. 87 5	WT8P
	6.3.17		" Hospital 28 nil	WT8P
			" D.R.S. 86 8	WT8P

WAR DIARY or INTELLIGENCE SUMMARY.

Army Form C. 2118.

(Erase heading not required.)

139TH FIELD AMBULANCE R.A.M.C.

Place	Date	Hour	Summary of Events and Information	Remarks and references to Appendices
Same	7.3.17		Remaining O.R. Hospital — Sick 28 — Wounded nil	WTSF
			" " D.R.S. — 89 — 9	
	8.3.17		" " Hospital — 25 — nil	
			" " D.R.S. — 85 — 8	
			Capt. J.W. MacDonald R.A.M.S. proceeded for temp duty to R.E. Head Qrs 38th Div.	WTSF
			— Sick — Wounded	
	9.3.17		Remaining O.R. Hospital — 31 — nil	
			" " D.R.S. — 95 — 7	QTSF
			aq A.D.M.S. visited Hospital & D.R.S.	WTSF
	10.3.17		Remaining O.R. Hospital — 35 — nil	
			" " D.R.S. — 89 — 2	
			" " Hospital — 33 — nil	
	11.3.17		" " D.R.S. — 89 unf 111 — 1 unf	WTSF
			Capt. T.Kelly. R.A.M.C. returned from temp duty as M.O. 19th Welch Regt.	
			Capt. J.T. O'Boyle. R.A.M.E. proceeded for temp duty with 10th Bat. Welch Regt.	WTSF
	12.3.17			

Army Form C. 2118.

WAR DIARY
or
INTELLIGENCE SUMMARY.

(Erase heading not required.)

Instructions regarding War Diaries and Intelligence Summaries are contained in F. S. Regs., Part II. and the Staff Manual respectively. Title pages will be prepared in manuscript.

Place	Date	Hour	Summary of Events and Information	Remarks and references to Appendices
Sarpi	12.3.17		Remaining O.R. Hospital Sick Wounded	
			39 nil	
			" " D.R.S. 89 1	
			4878 Sergt. T.M. Jones, R.A.M.C. of this Unit awarded the Italian Bronze Medal for military valour.	WT88.
	13.3.17		Remaining O.R. Hospital Sick Wounded	
			41 nil	
			" " D.R.S. 102 nil	WT88.
	14.3.17		" " Hospital 33 nil	
			" " D.R.S. 93 nil	WT88.
	15.3.17		" " Hospital 31 nil	
			" " D.R.S. 81 nil	WT88.
	16.3.17		" " Hospital 30 nil	
			" " D.R.S. 94 nil	WT88.
			A.D.M.S. visits site and examined T.U. & P.B. men.	
	17.3.17		Remaining O.R. Hospital 25 nil	
			" " D.R.S. 94	
			Capt. Walton, R.A.M.C. proceeded on leave. 2"Lt. J.H. Bankes, R.A.M.C. returned from Serapeum Outer or Canal Bank.	WT88.

WAR DIARY
or
INTELLIGENCE SUMMARY.

Army Form C. 2118.

Place	Date	Hour	Summary of Events and Information	Remarks and references to Appendices
Same	18.3.17		Capt. G.W. RIDDELL R.A.M.C proceeded on leave	
			Hospital 19 Sick wounded	
			Remaining O.R. Hospital 19 nil	W788
			" " D.R.S 97 nil	
			" " Hospital 17 nil	
			" " D.R.S. 92 nil	
	19.3.17		A.D.M.S. visited the site	W788
	20.3.17		Capt. J.T. O'BOYLE, R.A.M.C. returned from 10th Welch Regt.	
			Remaining O.R. Hospital 21 wounded	
			" " D.R.S 95 nil	W788
	21.3.17		" " Hospital 24 nil	
			" " D.R.S 92 nil	W788
	22.3.17		" " Hospital 20 nil	
			" " D.R.S 86 nil	W788
	23.3.17		" " Hospital 33 1	
			" " D.R.S. 88 nil	W788
			A.D.M.S. visited Site and inspected T.O. & P.B. men.	W788

Army Form C. 2118.

WAR DIARY
or
INTELLIGENCE SUMMARY.
(Erase heading not required.)

Instructions regarding War Diaries and Intelligence Summaries are contained in F. S. Regs., Part II. and the Staff Manual respectively. Title pages will be prepared in manuscript.

Place	Date	Hour	Summary of Events and Information				Remarks and references to Appendices
Same	24.3.17		Remaining	O.R.	Sick 25	wounded nil	WPS
	25.3.17		"	Hospital	99	4	
			"	D.R.S	27	nil	WPS
			"	Hospital	104	6	
	26.3.17		"	D.R.S	29	nil	WPS
			"	Hospital	93	6	
	27.3.17		"	D.R.S	29	nil	
			"	D.D.S	104	5	WPS
	28.3.17		"	Hospital	32	nil	2 Volunteers
			"	D.R.S	116	5	
			Colonel Saltau RAMC. Consulting Physician 2nd Army visited the Hospital.				M
	29.3.17		Remaining	O.R.	Sick 34	wounded nil	
				Hospital	97	6	M.
			Lieut Col W.B. EDWARDS RAMC granted leave 29-3-17 - 8-4-17				

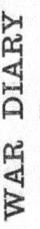

WAR DIARY
or
INTELLIGENCE SUMMARY.
(Erase heading not required.)

Army Form C. 2118.

Place	Date	Hour	Summary of Events and Information	Remarks and references to Appendices
Same	30.3.17		Remaining O.R. Sick – Wounded Hospital 35 – nil D.I.S. 98 5 D/MS 2nd Army accompanied by D/MS VIIIth Corps & D/MS 38th Division inspected Field Ambulance at D.R.S. and expressed himself as being very pleased with everything he had seen. Capt G.W. RIDDEL RAMC rejoined from leave	PD.
	31-3-17		Remaining O.R. Sick Wounded Hospital 26 – nil 95 5	PD.

F. Jawor Lees
Capt RAMC
O/C 129th Field Ambulance

Original.
April 9

War Diary.

129th Field Ambulance

April 1917

Stout
14/9/086

Vol 14

COMMITTEE FOR THE
MEDICAL HISTORY OF THE WAR
Date -6 JUN 1917

Army Form C. 2118.

WAR DIARY
or
INTELLIGENCE SUMMARY.
(Erase heading not required.)

129TH FIELD AMBULANCE
No. ....
Date ....

Instructions regarding War Diaries and Intelligence Summaries are contained in F.S. Regs., Part II. and the Staff Manual respectively. Title pages will be prepared in manuscript.

Place	Date	Hour	Summary of Events and Information	Remarks and references to Appendices
PROVEN. F 7 c 3.3	1/4/17		Remaining Hospital Sick 26 Wounded —	
			DRS 92 7	
	2"		Capt J.T. O'BOYLE R.A.M.C. proceeded 31/7/17 for temporary duty with 14th R.W.F.	
			Remaining Hospital Sick 32 Wounded —	
			DRS 92 6	
			Capt T. KELLY R.A.M.C. detailed to see morning sick of 'C' & 'D' Batteries Wagon Lines 276th Brigade R.F.A. at HOUTKERQUE daily from 2/4/17 - 12/4/17.	
	3"		Remaining Hospital Sick 35 Wounded —	
			DRS 92 7	
	4"		" Hospital 33	
			DRS 87 9	
	5"		" Hospital 32	
			DRS 76 10	

Army Form C. 2118.

WAR DIARY
or
INTELLIGENCE SUMMARY.

(Erase heading not required.)

129TH FIELD AMBULANCE
No. ....
Date ....

Instructions regarding War Diaries and Intelligence Summaries are contained in F.S. Regs., Part II. and the Staff Manual respectively. Title pages will be prepared in manuscript.

Place	Date	Hour	Summary of Events and Information	Remarks and references to Appendices
Same	6/4/17		Remaining Hospital — Sick 33 — Wounded — DRS 86 — 12	JR
	7/4/17		ADMS 38th (Welsh) Division visited Ambulance Site & examined suggested 28 TU new Remaining Hospital — Sick 33 — Wounded — DRS 81 — 11	M
	8/4/17		Hospital 36 — 6 DRS 95 — Capt F.P. REES RAMC attended conference of O i/c Field Ambulances 38th Division at ADMS Office. Lieut-Col W. BICKERTON EDWARDS RAMC rejoined from leave. Remaining Hospital Sept 28 — wounded — Nil DRS — 90 — 5	W. Bickerton Edwards Capt RAMC
	9/4/17		attended conference at 36th DRS. J&D Work. 2: J.H. BANKES RAMC proceeded to take over temp Sanitary Charge of Canal Bank. Capt. J.T. O'BOYLE RAMC returned from temp duty with 14th Bn RWF	W. Bickerton Edwards

2353 Wt. W2544/1454 700,000 5/15 D. D. & L. A.D.S.S./Forms/C. 2118.

Army Form C. 2118.

129TH FIELD AMBULANCE

WAR DIARY
or
INTELLIGENCE SUMMARY.
(Erase heading not required.)

Place	Date	Hour	Summary of Events and Information			Remarks and references to Appendices
Camp	10.4.17		Remaining	Hospital	Sick 23	wounded nil	
	11.4.17		"	D.R.S.	101	6	W.R.F.
				Hospital	29	nil	W.R.F.
	12.4.17		"	D.R.S.	84	5	W.R.F.
				Hospital	31	nil	
	13.4.17		"	D.R.S	94	4	W.R.F.
				Hospital	30	nil	
				D.R.S.	93	3	
			A.D.M.S. Inspected Hospital & D.R.S. Capt. T. KELLY. R.A.M.C. proceeded				W.R.F.
			for Temp: duty to 46 C.C.S.		sick	wounded	
	14.4.17		Remaining	Hospital	28	nil	W.R.F.
				D.R.S.	116	6	
	15.4.17		"	Hospital	29	nil	
				D.R.S.	97	3	
			Capt. R.G.H. WESTON. R.A.M.C. returned from leave. Capt. G.W. RIDDELL R.A.M.C. proceeded with advance to WORMHOUDT and took over Field Amb & D.R.S sites and also VIII Corps officers Rest Station from the 70th & 70th Field Ambulances.				W.R.F.

WAR DIARY
or
INTELLIGENCE SUMMARY.

(Erase heading not required.)

Army Form C. 2118.

129TH FIELD AMBULANCE

Place	Date	Hour	Summary of Events and Information	Remarks and references to Appendices
Proven	16.4.17		Remaining Hospital Sick Wounded 33 14 71	
WORMHOUDT C.16.b.b.7 Sheet 27	17.4.17		Field Amb & D.R.S site at PROVEN handed over to the 132nd Field Amb. Also 29 Pack vizt. 13 in D.R.S & 16 in Hospital. Remainder of personnel and transport of 129 Field Amb proceeded to WORMHOUDT. Patients taken over from 71st Field Amb. Hospital 11. D.R.S 57. 0 From the 70th Field Amb 8 Officers at C.C.S. Remaining Hospital Sick Wounded 26 mj 4 D.R.S 110 ml C.C.R.S. 12 Belgian Salonghein 1st Class Sergt George Jonnis proceeded for duty with the 131st Field Amb.	W.O.T WD83
	18.4.17		Remaining Hospital Sick Wounded 21 mj 3 D.R.S. 74 ml C.C.R.S. 11	WD88
	19.4.17		Capt F.T. REES. R.A.M.C granted contract leave 19.4.17 to 3.5.17	WD88

WAR DIARY
or
INTELLIGENCE SUMMARY.
(Erase heading not required.)

Army Form C. 2118.

Place	Date	Hour	Summary of Events and Information			Remarks and references to Appendices
Camp	19.4.17		Hospital	Sick	wounded	
			Remaining	20	nil	
			D.R.S "	49 "	"	W.T.P.
			C.O.R.S "	12 "	"	
	20.4.17		Hospital			
			Remaining	14	"	
			D.R.S. "	42	"	
			C.O.R.S.	10	"	W.T.P
	21.4.17		A.D.M.S. inspected Hospital	D.R.S & C.O.R.S	Wounded	
			Remaining Hospital	Sick	nil	
			D.R.S.	48	3	W.T.P
			C.O.R.S.	10	nil	
	22.4.17		Hospital	9		
			D.R.S	86	2	W.T.P
			C.O.R.S	10	0	
	23.4.17		Hospital	10	nil	
			D.R.S	78	3	W.T.P
			C.O.R.S	9	nil	

WAR DIARY
or
INTELLIGENCE SUMMARY.

Army Form C. 2118.

Place	Date	Hour	Summary of Events and Information	Remarks and references to Appendices
Same	24.4.17		Remaining Hospital 10 Sick nil wounded	
			D.R.S. 82 3	
			C.O.R.S. 11 nil	
			Bgd. Gen. ATKINSON. D.A. gng. VIII Corps inspected C.O.R.S.	W78F
25.4.17			Remaining Hospital 12 Sick 2 wounded nil	
			D.R.S. 72 nil	
			C.O.R.S. 8 nil	
26.4.17			" Hospital 12 nil	W78F
			D.R.S. 70 1	
			C.O.R.S. 8 nil	
27.4.17			" Hospital 14 1 nil	W78F
			D.R.S. 69 nil	
			C.O.R.S. 7 nil	
28.4.7.			" Hospital 16 nil	W78F
			D.R.S. 74 3	
			C.O.R.S. 10 nil	
			1 NCO & 24 Men proceeded for duty with the 130th Field Amb.	W78F

WAR DIARY
or
INTELLIGENCE SUMMARY.
(Erase heading not required.)

Army Form C. 2118.

Place	Date	Hour	Summary of Events and Information	Remarks and references to Appendices
Laure	29.4.17		Remaining. Hospital D.R.S. C.O.R.S.	Sick 20 88 13	Wounded nil 5 nil	nil
	30.4.17		A.D.M.S. inspected the Unit. Remaining. Hospital D.R.S. C.O.R.S.	21 86 14	nil 4 nil	

W. Kirkland Stevens
Lt. Colonel R.A.M.C.
O.C. 129th FIELD AMBULANCE,
38th (WELSH) DIVISION.

War Diary
of
129th Field Ambulance
May 1917

Original

Army Form C. 2118.

WAR DIARY
or
INTELLIGENCE SUMMARY.
(Erase heading not required.)

129TH FIELD AMBULANCE.
No............
Date............

Place	Date	Hour	Summary of Events and Information	Remarks and references to Appendices
Wormhoudt C.16 b.6.7 Sheet 27	1.5.17		Hospital Remaining O.R. Sick 30 Wounded 1	
			D.R.S. " " 89 3	
			C.O.R.S. " Officers 13 nil	
	2.5.17		Capt. R.H.G. WESTON R.A.M.C. proceeded to take over 134th Field Amb. Field Amb estd at BOLLEZELE on Apl 30th from the 134th Field Amb.	WD8
			Hospital Remaining O.R. Sick 36 Wounded nil	
			D.R.S. " O.R. 104 6	
			C.O.R.S. " Officers 12 nil	
	3.5.17		Lt. J.H. BANKES R.A.M.C returned from Temp. duty as Sanitary Officer on the Canal Bank. 1 NCO + 6 O.R. rejoined the Unit from Baths Esquelbecq. 4 other ranks returned from Drying Rooms. POPERINGHE.	WD8
			Hospital Remaining O.R. Sick 25 Wounded nil	
			D.R.S. " O.R. 101 6	
			C.O.R.S. " Officers 13 nil	
	4.5.17		Hospital " O.R. 20 nil	WD8
			D.R.S. " O.R. 90 5	
			C.O.R.S. " Officers 12 1	WD8

Army Form C. 2118.

WAR DIARY
or
INTELLIGENCE SUMMARY.
(Erase heading not required.)

129TH FIELD AMBULANCE.

Place	Date	Hour	Summary of Events and Information	Remarks and references to Appendices
Same	4.5.17		Capt. F.T. REES R.A.M.C. returned from leave. 5 O.R. rejoined unit from Divisional Baths	W7RF
	5.5.17		Hospital Remaining O.R. Sick 25 wounded nil	W7RF
			D.R.S. " O.R. " 95 " 9	
			C.O.R.S. " Officers " 11 " 1	
	6.5.17		Hospital " O.R. 26 " nil	
			" Officer 2 " nil	
			D.R.S. " O.R. 77 " 8	
			C.O.R.S. " Officers 10 " 1	
			Medical Board held on P.B. men. Members: Lt Col Edwards R.A.M.C., Capt REES R.A.M.C., Capt O'BOYLE R.A.M.C.	W7RF
	7.5.17		Hospital Remaining O.R. Sick 20 wounded nil	
			" Officer 3 " nil	
			D.R.S. " O.R. 80 " 7	
			C.O.R.S. " Officers 10 " 1	
			Lt J.H. BANKES R.A.M.C. attached to see the sick of N⁰ Sect. D.A.C. at HERZEELE	W7RF
			Medical Board held on 2/Lt Qm NORTON 11th S.W.B. A.D.M.S. notified	
			Hospital, D.R.S & C.O.R.S.	W7RF

Army Form C. 2118.

WAR DIARY
or
INTELLIGENCE SUMMARY.
(Erase heading not required.)

129TH FIELD AMBULANCE.

Place	Date	Hour	Summary of Events and Information			Remarks and references to Appendices
Serre	8.5.17		Hospital D.R.S. C.O.R.S.	Remaining O.R. Officers O.R. Officers	Sick 21 1 5 9	wounded nil nil 1 1	W7F5
	9.5.17		Hospital D.R.S. C.O.R.S.	O.R. Officers O.R. C.O.R.S.	24 2 75 9	nil nil 2 nil	W7F5
	10.5.17		Hospital D.R.S. C.O.R.S.	O.R. Officers O.R. C.O.R.S.	20 1 69 9	nil nil 1 nil	W7F2
	11.5.17		Hospital D.R.S. C.O.R.S.	O.R. O.R. O.R's	22 64 9	nil nil nil	W7F2
			Capt. J.T. O'BOYLE R.A.M.C. proceeded for Temp duty on m/c 17 Bn Northumberland Fus.				W7F8
	12.5.17		Hospital D.R.S. C.O.R.S.	Remaining O.R. O.R. Officers	Sick 32 69 8	wounded nil nil nil	3.W.N.i

WAR DIARY or INTELLIGENCE SUMMARY

129TH FIELD AMBULANCE

Army Form C. 2118.

Place	Date	Hour	Summary of Events and Information		Remarks and references to Appendices
Serinel	13/5/17		Hospital D.R.S. C.O.R.S.	Remaining O.R. " O.R. " Officers	Sick Wounded 27 nil 70 3 7 nil
	14/5/17		A.D.M.S. inspected Hospital, D.R.S., C.O.R.S. Hospital D.R.S. C.O.R.S.	Remaining O.R. " O.R. " Officers	24 nil 70 3 7 nil	W768
	15/5/17		Hospital D.R.S. C.O.R.S.	Remaining O.R. " O.R. " Officers	29 nil 67 3 7 nil	W768
	16/6/17		Hospital D.R.S. C.O.R.S.	Remaining O.R. " O.R. " Officers	36 nil 70 3 9 nil	W768
			10 O.R. returned from duty on the Canal Bank			W768
	17/5/17		Hospital D.R.S. C.O.R.S.	Remaining O.R. " O.R. " Officers	29 nil 93 9 9 1	W768

WAR DIARY
or
INTELLIGENCE SUMMARY.
(Erase heading not required.)

Army Form C. 2118.

129TH FIELD AMBULANCE.

Place	Date	Hour	Summary of Events and Information	Remarks and references to Appendices
Seninghem	17.5.17		Capt R.H.G.WESTON.RAMC. & 10 O.R. rejoined the Unit from BOLLEZEELE. 1 N.C.O. & 1 Pte left here as working party of Stationary Sick. 4 O.R. rejoined from COUTHOVE Laundry. A.D.M.S. inspected Hospital. D.R.S. & C.O.R.S	WD8
	18.5.17		Remaining O.R. Sick 33 Wounded nil	
			Hospital O.R. 95 8	
			D.R.S. Officers - 1	
			C.O.R.S.	WD
	19.5.17		Hospital O.R. 33 nil	
			D.R.S. O.R. 97 8	
			C.O.R.S. Officers 8 1	
			Capt J.J.O'BOYLE.RAMC rejoined from temp duty with 17 Br NORTHUMBERLAND Fus.	WD68
	20.5.17		Remaining O.R. 29 nil	
			Hospital O.R. 98 9	
			D.R.S. Officers - 1	
			C.O.R.S.	WD8
	21.5.17		Hospital Officers 4 nil	
			D.R.S. O.R. 84 7	
			C.O.R.S. Officers 1 1	
			Capt R.H.G.WESTON.RAMC. attached to take over duty as Sanitary Officer, Reserve Area	WD9

WAR DIARY
or
INTELLIGENCE SUMMARY.

(Erase heading not required.)

Army Form C. 2118.

129TH FIELD AMBULANCE.

Place	Date	Hour	Summary of Events and Information			Remarks and references to Appendices
Same	22.5.17		Hospital	O.R.	Sick 30	
			D.R.S.	O.R.	69	
			C.O.R.S.	Officers	10	
	23.5.17		Hospital	O.R.	32	4788
			D.R.S.	O.R.	91	
			C.O.R.S.	Officers	9	
	24.5.17		Proceeded at Medical board on P.B. & 74 men at COUTHOVE & Div. Strength. 4788
			Hospital	O.R.	32	nil
				Officers	1	nil
			D.R.S.	O.R.	90	3
			C.O.R.S.	Officers	10	1
			Capt T. KELLY RAMC returned to duty from 46 C.C.S.			4782
	25.6.17		Hospital	O.R.	36	nil
				Officers	1	nil
			D.R.S.	O.R.	107	3
			C.O.R.S.	Officers	9	1
			A.D.M.S. inspected Hospital, D.R.S. & C.O.R.S.			4788

Army Form C. 2118.

WAR DIARY
or
INTELLIGENCE SUMMARY.
(Erase heading not required.)

129TH FIELD AMBULANCE.
No..........
Date..........

Place	Date	Hour	Summary of Events and Information			Remarks and references to Appendices
				Sick	Wounded	
Somme	26.5.17	Hospital	Remaining	O.R.	22	nil
		D.R.S.	"	Others	1	nil
		C.O.R.S.	"	D.R.	114	3
				Others	9	1
	27.5.17	Hospital	"	O.R.	26	nil
		D.R.S.	"	Others	3	nil
		C.O.R.S.	"	O.R.	102	3
				Others	7	1
	28.5.17	Hospital	"	O.R.	26	nil
		D.D.S.	"	Others	20	nil
		C.O.R.S.	"	O.R.	9	2
				Officers	9	1
	29.5.17	Hospital	"	O.R.	32	nil
		D.D.S.	"	Others	3	nil
		C.O.R.S.	"	O.R.	9	2
				Officers	8	1
	30.5.17	Hospital	"	O.R.	56	nil
		Hospital		Others	1	nil
		D.R.S.		O.R.	104	3
		C.O.R.S.		Others	7	1

WAR DIARY or INTELLIGENCE SUMMARY

Army Form C. 2118.

Place	Date	Hour	Summary of Events and Information	Remarks and references to Appendices
Sanne	30/5/17		Coy T. KELLY R.A.M.C + an advance party of 2 NCOs + 3 men proceeded to ESQUERDES to take over Hospital Site occupied by NEW ZEALAND Field Amb.	W76.8
"	31/5/17			
			O.R. Sick Wounded	
			Hospital Remaining 28 nil	
			D.R.S. " officer - nil	
			C.O.R.S. " O.R. 122 2	
			officer 8 -	
			Capt F.T. REES R.A.M.C and remainder of party proceeded to ESQUERDES.	W78.8
			To open out a Hospital for pa/heads of 113 Brigade.	

W. Beckton Sawards
Lt Col R.A.M.C
O.P. 129th Field Amb Galance

Vol 16

146/230

WAR DIARY

129TH FIELD AMBULANCE

for Month of June 1917.

129TH FIELD AMBULANCE

COMMITTEE FOR THE
MEDICAL HISTORY OF THE WAR
Date: -7 AUG. 1917

ORIGINAL COPY

SECRET

B.E.F.

SUMMARY OF MEDICAL WAR DIARIES FOR

129th F.A. 38th Divn. 14th Corps, 5th Army.

WESTERN FRONT June 1917.

O.C. Lt. Col. W.B. Edwards.

SUMMARISED UNDER THE FOLLOWING HEADINGS.

Phase "D" Battle of Messines June 1917.

B.E.F. 1.

129th F.A. 38th Div. 14th Corps, 5th Army.   WESTERN FRONT
O.C. Lt. Col. W.B. Edwards.   June 1917.

Phase "D" Battle of Messines June 1917.

1917.	Headquarters. At Wormhoudt C.16.b.6.7.	(Sheet 27)
June 10th.	Transfer. Unit transferred with 38th Divn. from 8th Corps 2nd Army to 14th Corps, 5th Army.	
	Medical Arrangements: Unit running D.R.S. and C.O.R.S. Det. at Esquerdes for local sick.	
11th.	Moves Detachment: O and 5 rejoined Headquarters from Esquerdes.	
22nd.	Moves Detachment: Detachment at Esquerdes proceeded with 114th Bde. to Ledinghem.	
23rd.	Moves Detachment: O and 6 to Det. at Ledinghem.	
26th- 27th.	Moves Detachment: Det. from Ledinghem to La Tirmand.	
28th.	Medical Arrangements: D.R.S. and C.O.R.S. handed over to 89th Field Ambulance.	
	Moves Detachment: Det. from La Tirmand to Auchy-Au-Bois	
29th- 30th.	Moves: To Auchy- Au-Bois- Training Area.	

B.E.F.

SUMMARY OF MEDICAL WAR DIARIES FOR

129th F.A. 38th Divn. 14th Corps, 5th Army.

WESTERN FRONT June 1917.

O.C. Lt. Col. W.B. Edwards.

SUMMARISED UNDER THE FOLLOWING HEADINGS.

Phase "D" Battle of Messines June 1917.

B.E.F.

129th F.A. 38th Div. 14th Corps, 5th Army.   WESTERN FRONT
O.C. Lt. Col. W.B. Edwards.   June 1917.

Phase "D" Battle of Messines June 1917.

1917.	Headquarters. At Wormhoudt C.16.b.6.7. (Sheet 27)
June 10th.	Transfer. Unit transferred with 38th Divn. from 8th Corps 2nd Army to 14th Corps, 5th Army.
	Medical Arrangements: Unit running D.R.S. and C.O.R.S. Det. at Esquerdes for local sick.
11th.	Moves Detachment: O and 5 rejoined Headquarters from Esquerdes.
22nd.	Moves Detachment: Detachment at Esquerdes proceeded with 114th Bde. to Ledinghem.
23rd.	Moves Detachment: O and 6 to Det. at Ledinghem.
26th- 27th.	Moves Detachment: Det. from Ledinghem to La Tirmand.
28th.	Medical Arrangements: D.R.S. and C.O.R.S. handed over to 99th Field Ambulance.
	Moves Detachment: Det. from La Tirmand to Auchy-Au-Bois
29th- 30th.	Moves: To Auchy- Au-Bois- Training Area.

WAR DIARY or INTELLIGENCE SUMMARY.

Army Form C. 2118.

129TH FIELD AMBULANCE.

Place	Date	Hour	Summary of Events and Information	Remarks and references to Appendices
WORMHOUDT	1.6.17		Remaining Hospital Officers 2 Wounded nil	WRE
			" " O.R. 31 nil	
			D.R.S. O.R. 111 2	
			C.O.R.S. Officers 6 nil	
	2.6.17		Remaining Hospital Officers 2 nil	
			" " O.R. 34 nil	
			D.R.S. O.R. 92 4	
			C.O.R.S. Officers 6 nil	
	3.6.17		Lt. J.H. BANKES. R.A.M.C. proceeded on the 2nd 6.17 proceeded for temporary duty as the 1st Cap. J.W. MACDONALD R.A.M.C. at the 131st Field Am.B. Visited section of 129 Field Amb at ESQUERDES.	WRE
			Remaining Hospital Officers Sick Wounded	
			" " O.R. 28 nil	
			D.R.S. O.R. 80 4	
			C.O.R.S. Officers 9 nil	
	4.6.17		A.D.M.S 38th Welsh Division. Visited this side and inspected Hospital, D.R.S. & C.O.R.S.	WRE
			Remaining Hospital Officers Sick Wounded	
			" " O.R. 25 nil	
			D.R.S O.R. 63 4	
			C.O.R.S Officers 11 nil	WRE

WAR DIARY
or
INTELLIGENCE SUMMARY.
(Erase heading not required.)

Army Form C. 2118.

129TH FIELD AMBULANCE.

Place	Date	Hour	Summary of Events and Information			Remarks and references to Appendices
				Sick	Wounded	
Same	5.6.17		Remaining Hospital Officers	1	nil	
			" O.R's	30	nil	
			" O.R.S.	63	4	
			Officers	12	nil	6778
	6.6.17		Hospital Officers	1	nil	
			" O.R	29	nil	
			" O.R	70	7	
			D.R.S. Officers	10	nil	
			C.O.R.S. Officers			6778
			Officers conference of O.C's Field Ambulances at A.D.S.'s			
	7.6.17		Remaining Hospital Officers	1	nil	
			" O.R.S	31	nil	
			D.R.S	01	10	
			C.O.R.S Officers	11	nil	6778
			Visited section of New Ambulance at Engineers			
	8.6.17		Hospital Remaining Officers	1	nil	
			" O.R	36	nil	
			D.R.S	120	11	
			C.O.R.S Officers	12	nil	6778
			Ag. R.P.M.S. 38 "totes" transfer wailed to Lill and evacuated 98.7%			
			D.D.M.S. 8th Corps visited and inspected the site			

Army Form C. 2118.

129TH FIELD AMBULANCE
No. ....
Date ....

WAR DIARY
or
INTELLIGENCE SUMMARY.
(Erase heading not required.)

Instructions regarding War Diaries and Intelligence Summaries are contained in F. S. Regs., Part II. and the Staff Manual respectively. Title pages will be prepared in manuscript.

Place	Date	Hour	Summary of Events and Information	Remarks and references to Appendices
Sains	9.6.17		Hospital. Remaining Officers	Left	Wounded	
			D.R.S.	2	nil	
			C.O.R.S.	8	nil	
			Officers	121	13	
				12	nil	
			9' + Q.R. I Norley R.a.m.c. granted leave 9.6.17 to 19.6.17		
			47638 Corporal Harrison E.R. R.A.M.C. awarded military medal		4778
	10.6.17			Sick	Wounded	
			Remaining Hospital Officers	27	nil	
			"	1	nil	
			D.R.S. O.R.	123	12	
			C.O.R.S. Officers	12	nil	
	11.6.17		Remaining Hospital Officers	1	nil	4778
			" O.R.	30	nil	
			D.R.S. O.R.	112	18	
			C.O.R.S. Officers	12	nil	
			1 Sergt + 1 8 O.R. returned to this station from duty on the Canal Bank & were relieved by a similar number of NCO's + men.		4/788
			1 Sergt + 10 men returned to this station from duty at ESQUERDES		

2353 Wt. W2544/1454 700,000 5/15 D. D. & L. A.D.S.S./Forms/C. 2118.

WAR DIARY
or
INTELLIGENCE SUMMARY.
(Erase heading not required.)

Army Form C. 2118.

129TH FIELD AMBULANCE

Place	Date	Hour	Summary of Events and Information			Remarks and references to Appendices
JAMES	12.6.17		Remaining Hospital	O.R. 29	Sick wounded	
			D.R.S.	O.R. 103	nil	2788
			C.D.R.S.	Officers 13	nil	
	13.6.17		Remaining Hospital	O.R. 21	nil	
			D.R.S.	O.R. 121	19	2708
			C.D.R.S.	Officers 12	nil	
	14.6.17		Remaining Hospital	O.R. 18	nil	
			D.R.S.	O.R. 119	17	2788
			C.D.R.S.	Officers 12	nil	
			D.D.M.S. 18th Corps visited and inspected the C.D.R.S. M.S. & Hospital			
	15.6.17		Remaining Hospital	O.R. 27	nil	
			D.R.S.	O.R. 126	10	with
			C.D.R.S.	Officers 13	nil	
			A/D.D.M.S. 38th West Horseer visited & inspected the C.D.R.S. D.R.S. Hospital & also Sector at ESQUERDES.			

WAR DIARY
or
INTELLIGENCE SUMMARY.
(Erase heading not required.)

Army Form C. 2118.

129TH FIELD AMBULANCE.

Place	Date	Hour	Summary of Events and Information			Remarks and references to Appendices
Same	16.6.17		Remaining Hospital O.R.	29	forwarded	
			" D.R.S.	112	nil	
			" C.O.R.S	10	15	
					nil	W78.1
	17.6.17		Remaining Hospital O.R.	29	nil	
			D.R.S.	123	15	
			C.O.R.S. Officers	10	nil	
	18.6.17		D.M.S. 5th Army & Lt N.S. 4th Corps Inspected 145 C.O.R.S. D.R.S. & Hospital		nil	
			Remaining Hospital O.R.	21	nil	
			D.R.S.	115	16	
			C.O.R.S. Officers	8	nil	W78.2
			Hospital "	1	nil	
	19.6.17		Remaining Hospital Officers	1	nil	
			O.R.	28	nil	
			D.R.S. O.R.	114	12	
			C.O.R.S Officers	9	nil	W78.3

Army Form C. 2118.

129TH FIELD AMBULANCE.

WAR DIARY
or
INTELLIGENCE SUMMARY.
(Erase heading not required.)

Place	Date	Hour	Summary of Events and Information	Remarks and references to Appendices
Shuis E	20.6.17		Remaining Hospital O.R. 25 R.S.R.S. 104 Officers 11 Cy Opr twice R.A.M.C. Returned from leave. Capt. T. KELLY R.A.M.C. attached to attend 1st Field of 124 R.E. WATTEN. Remaining Hospital O.R. 28 R.S.R.S. 123 G.R.S. Officers 9	informed nil 13 nil nil 12 nil L.M.S.
	22.6.17		Proceeding on duty at ESQUERDES. Remaining Hospital O.R. 20 R.S.R.S. 108 C.R.S. Officers 9	nil 11 nil
	23.6.17		Exton was Capt. F.T. REES R.A.M.C. left ESQUERDES & proceeded with No. 8cH to LEDINGHEM in the WISMES area A.D.M.S. 38th Welsh Division with 1st Echelon P.B. Men. Admitted 1 Sergt & 8 O.R. sent to attachment at LEDINGHEM. Parties return at LEDINGHEM.	W.T.G.E.

WAR DIARY
or
INTELLIGENCE SUMMARY.
(Erase heading not required.)

Army Form C. 2118.

129TH FIELD AMBULANCE.

Place	Date	Hour	Summary of Events and Information			Remarks and references to Appendices
				Sick	Wounded	
Souri	23.6.17		Remaining Hospital O.R.	O.R. 26	nil	6785
			" O.R.	111	10.	
			C.O.R.S. Officers	7	nil	
	24.6.17		Hospital O.R.	O.R. 22	nil	6784
			D.R.S. O.R.	118	11	
			C.O.R.S. Officers	7	nil	
	25.6.17		Hospital O.R.	O.R. 20	nil	
			D.R.S. O.R.	121	13	
			C.O.R.S. Officers	7	nil	
			Proceeded with A.D.M.S. to AUCHY AU BOIS to inspect new hospital site.			678
			Transfer of Section at LEDINGHEM inspected to RECKLINGHEM.			
	28.6.17		Receiving. Hospital O.R.	O.R. 10	nil	
			D.R.S. O.R.	106	wounded nil	
			C.O.R.S. Officers	8	nil	6785
			Capt. F.J. REES. CAMC. injured with his section by tins in SACHIN. When he was informed by his Horse Transport			

WAR DIARY
or
INTELLIGENCE SUMMARY.

Army Form C. 2118.

129TH FIELD AMBULANCE.

Place	Date	Hour	Summary of Events and Information	Remarks and references to Appendices
Same	26.6.17		Major J.R. FIDDES R.H.M.C. with an advance party of the 89th Field Amb. arrived at WORMHOUDT. Running Hospital O.R. Sick 8 D.O.S O.R. 104 C.O.R.S. Officers 7 Wounded nil '' 11 Sick	3165
	27.6.17		Capt. J.T. REES R.A.M.C. and detachment proceeded to Lt. TIRMAN and N of LIGNY-LEZ-AIRES west of J.S.B. 142/3/B.F 2/C/B.F D.O.S. 4 O.R. 118 Remaining Hospital Officers 4 D.R.S. O.R. '' C.O.R.S. Officers Wounded nil '' nil Sick 8 '' nil	2765
	28.6.17		89th Field Amb. under the command of Lt. Col. T. FRASER R.A.M.C. arrived at WORMHOUDT at 6 A.M. At 2 p.m. the Hospital sde of F.R.S. & C.O.R.S at WORMHOUDT state handed over to the 89th Field Amb. The patients handover was as follows Hospital 1 Officer D.R.S. 83 O.R. C.O.R.S. 7 officers Capt. J.T. REES. R.A.M.C and advance 248.7. party proceeded to OUDEZY-au-BOIS.	248.7.

WAR DIARY
or
INTELLIGENCE SUMMARY.
(Erase heading not required.)

Army Form C. 2118.

129TH FIELD AMBULANCE

Place	Date	Hour	Summary of Events and Information	Remarks and references to Appendices
Same	29.6.17		Handed over Billets to 89th Field Amb.	
FERME DU LONGPOURTY W.21.6.7.8 Sheet 27			Unit proceeded by Bus to CAESTRE and billeted on the Farm at W.21.6.7.8 Sheet 27. Proceeded with Capt. O'BOYLE RAMC at 3pm to AUCHY-AU-BOIS. Reconn^g. Hospital nil. DRS OR 23.	A.T.B.E.
	30.6.17		Unit under Capt. G.W. RIDDEL RAMC proceeded at 6-30am to AUCHY-AU-BOIS and here at noon under the Horse transport of this Unit in charge of Capt. R.H.Q. WESTON RAMC. Arrived at AUCHY-AU-BOIS at 4-30 pm. Capt. F.T. REES + autochenil having handed over the Est. at 20. Turnard to the 130th Field Amb. reformed the 129th Field Amb. at 10 A.M. Capt. C.W. MacDONALD RAMC + Capt. J.H. BANKES RAMC returned this Unit. Together with the Sanitary section formed Company 12 OR, of 38th Welsh Division.	

W. Stroud for Lt.
Wm S. Smith

J. Bulgin Edwards
Lt. Colonel, R.A.M.C.
O.C. 129th FIELD AMBULANCE,
38th (WELSH) DIVISION.

WO 17
140/298

129th FIELD AMBULANCE
WAR DIARY.
JULY 1917.

COMMITTEE FOR THE
MEDICAL HISTORY OF THE WAR
Date   10 SEP.1917

Original copy.

129TH
FIELD
AMBULANCE.

WAR DIARY
or
INTELLIGENCE SUMMARY.

(Erase heading not required.)

Army Form C. 2118.

O⸺ 129 F.A Amb.

Place	Date	Hour	Summary of Events and Information	Remarks and references to Appendices
AUCHY AU BOIS	1.7.17		Evacuating Hospital O.R. Sick 1 wounded nil	
	2.7.17		In his Regr War'gs to discuss programme of Training	nil
	3.7.17		Col. T. KELLY R.A.M.C. proceeded 30.6.17 to duty as A.D.S. 16th. Div. Rcpt. Eqr. & Offs.	W.7.S
	4.7.17		Evacuating Hospital O.R. 7/8	nil nil nil
	5.7.17		" " " 22	W.7.S
			Quarterly Audit Board held on Unit Accts	
			Evacuating Hospital O.R. 38	nil W.7.S
			Lieut J.H. BARKES R.A.M.C granted contract leave 5.7.17 to 19.7.17	W.7.S W.7.S
	6.7.17		Evacuating Hospital O.R. 33	nil
	7.7.17		" " " 33	nil
	8.7.17		OC's conference attended at A.D.M.S" office	
			Evacuating Hospital O.R. 41	nil W.7.S
			Granted leave 9.7.17 to 19.7.17	W.7.S

WAR DIARY
or
INTELLIGENCE SUMMARY.
(Erase heading not required.)

O.C. 129 F^h Amb.

Army Form C. 2118.

Place	Date	Hour	Summary of Events and Information	Remarks and references to Appendices
AUCHY AU BOIS	9/7		Remaining O.R. Sick 39.	4 Men C/o Rheu
	10/7		Remaining O.R. Sick 36	PM
	11/7		Remaining O.R. Sick 36. Col J.E.H. Davies R.A.M.C. and Capt A. Jones R.A.M.C. D.A.D.M.S. examined men for P.B. A.D.M.S. Staff met all Battn MO's + Field Amb bearer officers in conference	PM
	12/7		Remaining O.R. Sick 32. Bearer Divisions of the three Field Ambulances took part in 30th Divisional Field day on training ground.	PM
	13/7		Remaining O.R. Sick 13	PM
	14/7		Remaining O.R. Sick 10. MSHs – Bdrms wet bearer officers of the three field Ambces in conference. Capt J. O'Boyce R.A.M.C. examined men employed at brigade HdQrs + identific team.	PM

B.E.F.

129th F.A. 38th Divn. 14th Corps, 5th Army: WESTERN FRONT

O.C. Lt. Col. W.B. Edwards.   July '17.

Phase "D" 1. Passchendaele Operations July-Nov. '17.
(a) Operations commencing 1st July 1917.

1917.

	Headquarters. At Auchy Au. Bois.
July 16th- 18th.	Moves: To Proven via Steenbecque and Hondeghem.
20th.	" To Coppernolle Farm.

Medical Arrangement: A.D.Ss. at Sussex Farm, Fusilier Farm and St. Johns on Canal Bank and two R.A.Ps. taken over from 88th Field Ambulance.

22nd. Casualties R.A.M.C. Capt. J.W. Macdonald and 4 O.Rs wounded on Canal Bank.

23rd. Casualties R.A.M.C. 0 and 1 died of wounds.
0 and 1 wounded.

24th. 0 and 2 wounded 0 and 2 gassed.
Casualties A.S.C. attached. 0 and 2 killed 0 and 1 W.

25th. Casualties R.A.M.C. Gas. 0 and 1 gassed.

27th. Moves To A.D.S. Sussex Farm.
Casualties: Few wounded admitted.
Casualties R.A.M.C. 0 and 2 wounded.

30th. Medical Arrangements: 2 and 84 from 130th Field Ambulance and 1 and 75 from 131st Field Ambulance arrived for duty during operations.
Casualties R.A.M.C Gas. 0 and 1 gassed.

31st. Operations. Attack commenced 3.50 a.m.

B.E.F.   1.

129th F.A. 38th Divn. 14th Corps, 5th Army: WESTERN FRONT

O.C. Lt. Col. W.B. Edwards.   July '17.

Phase "D" 1. Passchendaele Operations July-Nov. '17.

(a) Operations commencing 1st July 1917.

1917.	Headquarters. At Auchy Au. Bois.
July 16th- 18th.	Moves: To Proven via Steenbecque and Hondeghem.
20th.	" To Coppernolle Farm.
	Medical Arrangement: A.D.Ss. at Sussex Farm, Fusilier Farm and St. Johns on Canal Bank and two R.A.Ps. taken over from 88th Field Ambulance.
22nd.	Casualties R.A.M.C. Capt. J.W. Macdonald and 4 O.Rs wounded on/Canal Bank.
23rd.	Casualties R.A.M.C. 0 and 1 died of wounds. 0 and 1 wounded.
24th.	0 and 2 wounded 0 and 2 gassed.
	Casualties A.S.C. attached. 0 and 2 killed 0 and 1 W.
25th.	Casualties R.A.M.C. Gas. 0 and 1 gassed.
27th.	Moves To A.D.S. Sussex Farm.
	Casualties: Few wounded admitted.
	Casualties R.A.M.C. 0 and 2 wounded.
30th.	Medical Arrangements: 2 and 84 from 130th Field Ambulance and 1 and 75 from 131st Field Ambulance arrived for duty during operations.
	Casualties R.A.M.C Gas. 0 and 1 gassed.
31st.	Operations. Attack commenced 3.50 a.m.

B.E.F. 2.

<u>129th F.A. 38th Divn. 14th Corps, 5th Army.</u> WESTERN FRONT
<u>O.C. Lt. Col. W.B. Edwards.</u> July-Aug. '17.

Phase "D"1(a)   (Cont.)

1917.

July 31st,(Cont.) <u>Casualties Evacuation:</u>   wounded arrived at A.D.S. at 5 a.m. Cases from St. John and Fusilier A.D.Ss. cleared to road by trolley and thence by wheeled stretcher to A.D.S. Sussex Farm. No difficulty in clearing. Tram line to R.A.Ps broken and could not be used. Tramline repaired later and cases brought down by trolley. Large numbers of wounded cleared during the day.

<u>Medical Arrangements:</u>   2 and 168 of Divn. Train T.M.B, and Dinvl. Headquarters used as auxilary brs. St John A.D.S. closed 4 p.m.

R.A.Ps established at Iron Cross, Jolie Farm, and Stray Farm by 4 p.m.

<u>Casualties R.A.M.C.</u>   Capt. Evans attached 11th S.W.B. wounded, O and 6 wounded.

B.E.F.

129th F.A. 38th Divn. 14th Corps, 5th Army. WESTERN FRONT

O.C. Lt. Col. W.B. Edwards. July-Aug. '17

Phase "D" 1(a) (Cont.)

1917.

July 31st,(Cont.) Casualties Evacuation: wounded arrived at A.D.S. at 5 a.m. Cases from St. John and Fusilier A.D.Ss. cleared to road by trolley and thence by wheeled stretcher to A.D.S. Sussex Farm. No difficulty in clearing. Tram line to R.A.Ps broken and could not be used. Tramline repaired later and cases brought down by trolley. Large numbers of wounded cleared during the day.

Medical Arrangements: 2 and 168 of Divn. Train T.M.B, and Dinvl. Headquarters used as auxilary brs. St John A.D.S. closed 4 p.m.

R.A.Ps established at Iron Cross, Jolie Farm, and Stray Farm by 4 p.m.

Casualties R.A.M.C. Capt. Evans attached 11th S.W.B. wounded, O and 6 wounded.

WAR DIARY
or
INTELLIGENCE SUMMARY.

(Erase heading not required.)

O.C. 129 F/Amb.

Instructions regarding War Diaries and Intelligence Summaries are contained in F. S. Regs., Part II. and the Staff Manual respectively. Title pages will be prepared in manuscript.

Place	Date	Hour	Summary of Events and Information	Remarks and references to Appendices
Same	15/7		Remaining Hosp. OR. 10. Capt R.H. O'KIESTON + 6 OR proceeded as advance park to STEENBECQUE	OM
STEENBECQUE	16/7		Remaining Hosp. OR ? Unit & transport moved from AUCHY-AU-BOIS to STEENBECQUE Capt R.H.O. WESTON & advance park proceeded to HONDEGHEM.	OM
HONDEGHEM	17/7		Remaining Hosp OR ? Unit & transport moved to farm near HONDEGHEM. Remained one night Capt R.H.O. WESTON & advance park proceeded to P5 area PROVEN.	OM
PROVEN	18/7		Remaining Hosp OR 14. Unit & transport moved to P5 area PROVEN.	OM
"	19/7		Remaining Hosp OR 10. Capt J.W. MACDONALD R.AM.C. & Capt O'BOYLE R.AM.C. with 36 OR proceeded to	OM

WAR DIARY
or
INTELLIGENCE SUMMARY.   O.C. 129 Fd Amb.
(Erase heading not required.)

Place	Date	Hour	Summary of Events and Information	Remarks and references to Appendices
PROVEN	19/7		CANADA FARM as Advance Park & thence to A.D.S's on CANAL BANK. Lieut Col W.E.EDWARDS RAMC & Lieut J.H BANKES RAMC reported from leave.	22R. Manchester Cape RAMC
COPPERNOLLE	20/7		Remaining OR Sick 9. ADS's at SUSSEX FARM, FUSILIER FM, & ST JOHNS. on CANAL BANK and two BATTLE AID [illegible] at SUSSEX FARM. Mules came from 88th Fld Amb. Unit & Transport moved to COPPERNOLLE FARM. 1 N.C.O. & 18 O.R. proceeded for duty on Canal Bank.	M
"	21/7		Remaining OR sick Nil.	M
"	22/7		1 N.CO. & 12 O.R. proceeded for duty on CANAL BANK. Capt J.W MACDONALD RAMC, 1 Sergt & 3 O.R. wounded on CANAL BANK	M
"	23/7		Capt G.W RIDDEL RAMC proceeded to CANAL BANK. 1 Private died of wounds received in action and 1 Private wounded	M

WAR DIARY or INTELLIGENCE SUMMARY

Army Form AMBULANCE
129 Fd Amb.

Place	Date	Hour	Summary of Events and Information	Remarks and references to Appendices
Same	24/7	9am	Capt F.T. REES RAMC proceeded to CANAL BANK. Two A.S.C. Drivers killed in Action. 1 A.S.C. Sgt wounded. 2 RAMC Privates wounded and 2 gassed. 1 N.C.O. & 10 men proceeded to CANAL BANK for duty.	M
"	25/7		1 RAMC Private gassed	M
"	26/7		Lt Col W.B. EDWARDS RAMC evacuated sick to 62 CCS. Capt A JONES, M.O. 2/5 RWF took over temporary command of the Unit.	Marcake
	27/7/17		Under instructions from AD M.S. took over temporary command of this Unit. Warning order received from AD M.S. for medical units to be prepared to take up battle positions at short notice. Proceeded to Canal Bank and Field Bankes and reconnoitred positions and established A.D.S. of the unit at Groove A.D.S. Buses attached to MO's 15 Welsh & 15 RWF who occupied the right & left Battle and Fort respectively. Patrols sent out at 5 pm from these Battns to reconnoitre enemy lines — few casualties admitted.	Arrive

WAR DIARY or INTELLIGENCE SUMMARY.

(Erase heading not required.)

O C 129 Fd Amb

Place	Date	Hour	Summary of Events and Information	Remarks and references to Appendices
SUSSEX A D S Shaft 28 C 19 C 2.6	29/7/17		Capt R.A.G. Wroten R.A.M.C. attached to this unit proceeded for duty at A.D.M.S. office. 48273 Pte G Foley was to No. 4 C.C.S. P.U.O. 48042 Pte J.B. Willard wounded at duty. 48858 Pte S. Limbertone refs G.S.W. (Rec't Shillings)	A.J.
"	29/7/17		Visited A D S Stebmo at Trosbus and St John or Canal Bank - equipment for return operations sligentred to those places. 48914 Pte J.B. Jupp admitted 131 F.A. and P.U.O. 48677 " J. Wilkinson " " ashby	A.J.
"	29/7/17		Continued with preparations for offensive. Parties sent to Battle Aid Posts to strengthen them with logs etc. Various places at the various A.D.S. 48301 Pte Y. P. Thomas admitted 131. F.A. with P.U.O. 2 Officers (Capt J Banks & Lieut M. Gill) 3 N.C.O's and 81 O.R. reported from 130 Fd Amb. 1 " (Capt E.L. Reynolds) 3 N.C.O's and 72 O.R. reported from 131 F.Amb. Capt Wallace (M. O. 19 West), Capt Hepburn (M. O. Dac) Capt McMillan (M.O. Ham) reported for duty. Remainder of personnel of 129 F.A. arrived on Canal Bank. Orders issued to M.O's and N.C.O's with reference to their respective duties.	A.J.
"	30/7/17		All ranks paid to the various A D Stations & Battle aid pots. Ambulance wagons to M O C 115 CSM and ref. to picking up ramb bearers. 48021 Pte R.D. Jones admitted 131 F.A. (Burned Shell Gun Factory.)	A.J.

WAR DIARY
or
INTELLIGENCE SUMMARY.
(Erase heading not required.)

O C 129. Fd Amb

Place	Date	Hour	Summary of Events and Information	Remarks and references to Appendices
Shet 28 C 19 c 26	31/7/17	3-50 a.m.	Advance commenced. Evacuation arrived at A.D.S. at 5 a.m.	
		6 a.m.	Tramcar team, 2 Officers & 110 O.R. of T.M.B. reported for duty on trams at 6-30 am	
		7 a.m.	Amb cars arrived with wounded. Proposals to evacuate cases direct from St John and Trailers. Cases from ST JOHN cleared by trolley to road & cases from Trailer dumps & wheeled shelter carried near from there to evacuating cars to Duroix. No difficulty in clearance. Transfer to trestle and foot broken & ambulant trained.	
		8 a.m.	Right trenches repaired by R Amb and trollies sent up to B.A.P. Forward O.C. 151 coy R.E. & he detailed men by pm left tramline.	
		10 a.m.	R Amb called in at 130 Fd Amb.	
		12 a m	Cars delayed owing to Ottomans on traffic on road.	
		2 pm	Cases arrived. Left tramline repaired & trollies sent up to Left Bank A.P. Unofficially reported that M.O. 17 RWF wounded — RAMC notified & Capt Grove 130 Fd Amb sent to replace him.	
		3 pm	Capt Day, M.O. 15th RWF established outpost near him Croc owing to casualties in O.17 RWF. 18 M.O. 17 RWF went transport at Conn House.	A.J.

INTELLIGENCE SUMMARY

OC 129 Fd Amb.

Place	Date	Hour	Summary of Events and Information	Remarks and references to Appendices
C.19626	31/7/17	4 p.m.	Advanced Corps waited & went with him to Frezlin. Lt John Hope closed down owing to diversion of casualties to Frezlin. Th O.C. 1/4 & 1/5 Battns West Rgt established advanced aid post near JOLIE FARM & afterwards advanced to near STRAY FARM. Capt Evans M.O. 11 S.W.B. brought to A.D.S. wounded with both thighs & reported that a number of casualties were near Thinkerk & had not been cleared. Lt/Col ATTM.S. Whitfield reported that M.O. 10 S.W.B. wounded. Raining. The following casualties in personnel occurred: – 48739 Pte F.L. Bradford S.W.; 48305 Pte J.P. Evans S.W.; 48038 Pte R.N. Thomas S.W., 48325 Pte E. Clements S.W.; 48043 Pte A. Williams S.W.; 81168 Pte J.H. Bandry S.W. Large numbers of casualties cleared during the day. Carrying becoming arduous owing to length of advance and to the broken up condition of the ground in the captured territory.	

R Jones Capt
OC 129 Field Ambulance

WAR DIARY

129 Field Ambulance.

August 1917

Original Copy

B.E.F.

SUMMARY OF MEDICAL WAR DIARIES FOR
129th F.A., 38th Div., 14th Corps, 5th Army.

WESTERN FRONT JUNE.-SEPT. 1917.

O.C. Lt. Col. W.B. Edwards.

SUMMARISED UNDER THE FOLLOWING HEADINGS.

Phase "D" 1 Passchendaele Operations July-Nov. 1917
(a) Operations commencing 1st July 1917.

WAR DIARY or INTELLIGENCE SUMMARY

Army Form C. 2118.

O.C. 129 Fd Amb.

Place	Date	Hour	Summary of Events and Information	Remarks and references to Appendices
C19c2.6 (Sheet 28)	1/8/17	6 a.m	Lieut. McAllister RAMC 131 Fd Amb. reported for duty with 11th SWB. Sent bearer party with supplies & medical stores with him to two aid post established in front of STRAY FARM. Heavy Rain.	A.
		10 a.m.	Capt J.E. Davies RAMC 131 Fd Amb reported for duty with 10th SWB. Bearer party accompanied him to the Batt HQ. Position of Regtl M.O's as under:—	
			IRON CROSS POST ⊕ → M.O 15 RWF on Rt of IRON CROSS ⊕ M.O. 11 SWB ⊕ M.O 10 SWB	
			CORNER HOUSE ⊕ → M.O 17 RWF M.O 16 WELSH STRAY FARM ⊕ → M.O 14 Welsh	
			Lt BATTLE AID POST ⊕ → M.O 13 RWF, 14″, 16″. Rt B.A.P ⊕ M.O 10 Welsh, 13″	
			RAMC bearers relieved from each R.A.P. Few casualties coming down from right so majority of bearers sent up to CORNER HOUSE. Arms etc. Heavy rain made carrying mud arduous & necessitated 8 men to a stretcher.	
		12 noon	Sent rations, brandy, dressings, ammunition etc. up to each Regt aid post.	

WAR DIARY or INTELLIGENCE SUMMARY.

Army Form C. 2118.

(Erase heading not required.)

O-C 129 Fd Amb

Place	Date	Hour	Summary of Events and Information	Remarks and references to Appendices
Canal Bank Swamp A D S C19 c 2.6	1/8/17	4 p.m	Passed XIV Corps round ADS after having been to IRON CROSS. The clearance the possibility of establishing relay posts also as to feasibility of many roads running through the area by the left Divn. I considered impossible either to establish relay posts on the left or traverse any other means of clearance other than hand carriage. The roads between the canal and r communications were absolutely destroyed. 73318 Pte O.S. Widdowson & 64155 Pte J Waller admitted sick to No 4 Fd. Amb.	R.S.
do	2/8/17		Proceeded to CORNER HOUSE & IRON CROSS. Progress being made with wooden road from BARD CAUSEWAY to HUDDLESTON ROAD but owing to haystacks it was not fit for wheeled stretcher carriers. Ground between HUDDLESTON ROAD & CORNER HOUSE in a pitiable condition difficult to navigate. Road from Corner House to IRON CROSS in fair order - it had a hard surface & carrying not difficult. Majority of Bearers would be drawn from CORNER HOUSE to Canal Bank. Proposed Aid posts as under :—	

IRON CROSS PosT. ⊕ M.O. 15 R.W.F. ⟶ new Straytram ⊕ M.O. 14 Wchl
                                                                    15
CORNER HOUSE ⊕ M.O. 13 R.W.F ⟶ CANDLE TRENCH ⊕ M.O. 10 zuro
              16 wchl   ↓
                                   ↓
Lt B.A.P ⊕ M.O 14 R.W.F   Rt B.A.P ⊕ M.O 10 wchl
                                                      13
                                                  11 zuro.

WAR DIARY
or
INTELLIGENCE SUMMARY.

(Erase heading not required.)

Army Form C. 2118.

Place	Date	Hour	Summary of Events and Information	Remarks and references to Appendices
Canal Bank SWAMI A.D.S. C.19.c.2.6	2/8/17		The day was mostly on R.A.P's owing to events but the accommodation was limited. Capt Rice & amb ambce reconnoissance of area to the left of Cormon House but no signs of mules found. Capt Doyy M.O. 1/S.R.W.F went out to the STEENBEEK to plan wounded left by 115" B'de. R.E's commenced to extend Glengyle duckboard tramline to road junction at "5 Chemins Estaminet". Raining. Few casualties coming from STRAY FARM.	A.J.
do	3/8/17		48625 Pte R. McKnight admitted ac 130 F. Amb. Weather still bad. Visited outposts at night. Following part of R.A.M.C. kept there. Rapid progress being made with tram line on the right. Further progress made with northern road from BARD CAUSEWAY & duckboard track commenced towards CORNER HOUSE. Evacuation of casualties continued. Arms called.	A.J.
do	4/8/17		46958 Pte R. May admitted ac to 131 F. Amb. Weather improved - sunshine. Casualties only coming from left. So different channels of evac as all limbers available for the left & funk-road coming in. Morale calm. O.C. 61 F. Amb. & several officers called to ascertain routes of evacuation etc. Northern road completed as far as HUDDLESTON RD & duckboard track laid up to trench 500 yards from CORNER HOUSE. Glengyle duckboard tramline laid as far as GALLWITZ FARM. Casualties continued to be cleared from left.	A.J.

WAR DIARY
or
INTELLIGENCE SUMMARY.

(Erase heading not required.)

Army Form C. 2118.

O.C. 129 Fd Amb.

Place	Date	Hour	Summary of Events and Information	Remarks and references to Appendices
CANAL BANK	5/8/17	8 a.m.	Fine weather. Obtained reinforcements from left front.	
SUSSEX RD.		10 a.m.	Forward posts handed over to personnel from 61 Field Amb.	
C.N.C.2.6		12 noon	Bearers of 131 Fd Amb and returned to CANADA FARM.	
		2 p.m.	Handed over Advance Dressing Station Q.6 61 Fd Amb.	
			Gradually relieved all bearers to their units.	
		6 p.m.	Returned wounded returned to their units. Capt Riddell sent into reinforcement to PROVEN.	
COPPERNOLLE		9 p.m.	Returned wounded unit to COPPERNOLLE. Capt W. Brown joined unit for duty.	AA
			Invalid A.D.M.S. Office.	
			48752 Pte R May returned from hospital.	
COPPERNOLLE	6/8/17	8 a.m.	Unit moved to PROVEN AREA by road march and encamped at Shed 27 E.18.c.4.5. Special	
PROVEN		10 a.m.	hospital for sick. 20 patients admitted. Capt J O'Boyle detailed for duty as M.O. 16 details.	
			Rpt and strength off strength of Unit. Attached to the command of the unit.	
			48914 Pte B. Joyce + 48977 Pte J Welkman rejoined unit from hospital.	
do	7/8/17	-	Capt Beckman struck off strength, being posted as M.O. R.E.	AA
			H. A. Carlton joined for duty from 131 Fd Amb. Remaining in hospital 6.	
			48665 Pte R Murkinght rejoined unit from hospital.	
do	8/8/17	-	Various appts. Capt H Brown detailed to visit A.S.C Companies & D.A.D.S daily.	AA
			Classes under Lieut-Col whilst remained of 129 Fd Amb.	
			Remaining in hospital 11.	AA

WAR DIARY
or
INTELLIGENCE SUMMARY.

O.C. 129 Fd Amb.

Place	Date	Hour	Summary of Events and Information	Remarks and references to Appendices
PROVEN	9/8/17		Sent inspection unfit men.	
do	10/8/17		G.O.C. 38 Div. visited & approved the arrangements of the establishment of the advanced dressing station at Pelissier Fm. Toured Div HQ. 12 reinforcements joined. Remaining in hospital 17.	
do	11/8/17		Commenced the answering of various sundry installments.	
do	12/8/17		Submitted nominations for awards to DDMS. Capt J.R. Barks proceeded for duty as M.O. 16 RWF vice Lieut J.M. Adam RAMC who joined this unit. 6 reinforcements joined.	
do	"		48766 Pte A.R. Pritchard was wounded Cat., 316 9 S Ph 15 Whittington drive over to CCS gun shot head.	
do	13/8/17		Visited R.E.S. and QM to obtain supplies for further Openshaw.	
do	14/8/17		6 ORs proceeded for duty at Coy W.N.C.P. at MOUTON FARM	
do	15/8/17		488 Pte A. Hadden & 48656 Pte J.P. Sheels awarded Military Medal by Corps Commander	
do	16/8/17		5 reinforcements joined. Attended conference at Corps HQ on ground to STEEN BEEKE, IRON CROSS str and MAMUR & OC 130 Fd Amb. Lieut Dobson & P3 OR sent PELISSIER FARM to advance party	
do	17/8/17		6 ORs returned from CWW CP (MOUTON FARM)	

B.E.F. 3.

129th F.A. 38th Divn. 14th Corps, 5th Army. WESTERN FR

O.C. Lt. Col. W.H. Edwards. Aug.-Sept.

Phase "D" 1.(a) (Cont.)

1917.

Aug. 27th.   Operations. Bombardment commenced.

Operations Enemy. Gas shells on area.

Aug. 5th.	Moves:	To Coppernolle.
" 6th.	"	To E.18.b.4.5.(27) Proven.
16th.	Decorations.	Ptes Haddan and Dadd awarded M.M.
18th.	Moves:	To Pelissier Farm.
20th.	Decorations:	Pte. Smith and Dr. Jones awarded M.M.
23rd.	"	Capt. Rees awarded M.C. and Sgt. Thomas M.M.
26th.	Medical Arrangements:	Solferino established and equipped as A.D.S.

Aug. 5th.	Moves:	To Coppernolle.
6th.	"	To E.18.b.4.5.(27) Proven.
16th.	Decorations.	Ptes Haddan and Dadd awarded M.M.
18th.	Moves:	To Pelissier Farm.
20th.	Decorations:	Pte. Smith and Dr. Jones awarded M.M.
23rd.	"	Capt. Rees awarded M.C. and Sgt. Thomas M.M.
26th.	Medical Arrangements:	Solferino established and equipped as A.D.S.

B.E.F.   3.

<u>129th F.A. 38th Divn. 14th Corps, 5th Army.</u> <u>WESTERN FRONT</u>
<u>O.C. Lt. Col. W.H. Edwards.</u>   <u>Aug.-Sept.'17</u>

<u>Phase "D" 1.(a) (Cont.)</u>

1917.

Aug. 27th.   <u>Operations</u>. Bombardment commenced.

<u>Operations Enemy</u>. Gas shells on area.

WAR DIARY
or
INTELLIGENCE SUMMARY.
(Erase heading not required.)

O.C. 129 Fd Amb

Army Form C. 2118.

Place	Date	Hour	Summary of Events and Information	Remarks and references to Appendices
PROVEN	18/8/17	5 pm	Transport & Amb proceed under Capt W BROWNE to PELISSIER FARM	
PELISSIER FARM	do	7 am	Orderlies not mounting front to PELISSIER FARM	
		6 am	Arrived unit.	
			Capt RUSS 19 OR proceed to CHEAPSIDE to reinf ADS. walking wounded Collecting post, also dug out ADV DRESG FARM from 62 Fd Amb.	
			Capt RIDDEL 9 OR took over Evac. post Collecting post's CANADA FARM from 60 Fd Amb.	
			Capt BROWN + 33 OR proceed to Hand Bank Fr Auby and 130 Fd Amb	
			Name works. No 61 Fd Amb not moving out of PELISSIER FARM.	
do	19/8/17		Capt W Brown proceed for temporary duty as M.O. 10" Laws. Lieut Brabun reported	
			to O.C. 130 Fd Amb for temporary duty. Capt H Caldson proceed to CHEAPSIDE	
			Walk Evac. Sick Collecting post to accompanf arrangements could be made to return our	
			then had conducted march-in. Recommence opening up line for sick + ASD	
			evacuated.	
do	20/8/17		069655 Dr T J Jones, 102806 Pte T J Smith awarded military medal.	
			Sick admitted to hospital opened on this site.	
do	21/8/17		Aprnd reports Lieut Brabun returned from duty with 130 Fd Amb. 64810 Pte J Dram evac. sick.	
do	22/8/17		Picard to Chippawa. Progress being made there in informing the site.	
			10 4 24 8 Pte W Weddell evac. are to M 4 CCS	

WAR DIARY
or
INTELLIGENCE SUMMARY.
(Erase heading not required.)

O.C. 129 Fd Amb.

Army Form C. 2118.

Place	Date	Hour	Summary of Events and Information	Remarks and references to Appendices
PELISSIER FARM	23/8/17		4 reinforcements joined. Capt Rue awarded Military Cross. 48038 Sgt B Thomas awarded military medal.	Af
do	24/8/17		Lieut R.G. Binns joined for duty from 23rd FA? APMS examined unfit him. Proceeded to make reconnaissance of light railway in forward area with view to putting trams for wounded. Visited DHTHQ & later interviewed O/C Light Railways. 64828 Pte J Ritman, 59352 Pte A Wareham were wounded. 48388 Sgt C Edmonds was sick.	Af
do	25/8/17	5 am	Proceeded with 5 O.R along light railway line to terminus at BROAD ST. [near GALLWITZ FARM] walking wounded others placed along track leading from STRAY FARM to GALLWITZ T along track from CORNER HOUSE to GALLWITZ, also a road leading from HUDDLESTON RD to CHEAPSIDE. Left Khakis at dressing station at GALLWITZ. Visited ADMS Conference held at ADMS Office a.m. of practise. It was decided that O.C. 129 Fd Amb should open an ADS at GALLWITZ (C8a9?) that wounded should open a dressing station at SOLFERINO siding (shed 28 B23a05) that wounded should be cleared from the former to the latter by light railway. 33277 Pte J Taylor was wounded. 48820 Pte STR Toffen was sick.	
do	26/8/17		Inspected site at SOLFERINO & commenced to erect dressing tent D.	Af
do	27/8/17		Equipped SOLFERINO as a dressing station. Capt Carlisle & Lieut Binns sent to reconnoitre with necessary personnel. Made final arrangements for railway trials. Ramy Rainly.	Af

WAR DIARY or INTELLIGENCE SUMMARY.

Army Form C. 2118.

(Erase heading not required.)

O.C. 129 Ft Amb.

Place	Date	Hour	Summary of Events and Information	Remarks and references to Appendices
PELISSIER FARM	27/8/17	1-30 a.m.	Proceeded to ELVERDINGHE to No 1 Light Railway Officer.	
		1-55	Bombardment commenced.	
		2-30	Proceeded with 2 tractor 74 trucks each capable of accommodating 8 stretcher cases to GALLWITZ FARM. Rain continued.	
GALLWITZ FARM ADS	do	4-0	Arrived at GALLWITZ. A/W Andrew established there &. Bearers. Rd dumps repaired.	
	do	4-30 a.m.	A.D.M.S. 41st Division relieved. Sent to STRAY FARM to see that roads properly flagged.	
do	do	6-30 a.m.	Wounded commenced to arrive.	
	do	7 p.m.	4 lying cases & 24 sitting taken on train. Slightly wounded dropped near CHEAPSIDE, the remainder taken on to SOLFERINO, arriving there 7-30 p.m.	
SOLFERINO	do	7-45	Left with empty train to ADS	
GALLWITZ	do	8-30	Arrived. Waited for 10 minutes & dispatched 5 lying & 8 sitting cases on train in charge of an Officer. No cases at Gallwitz so drew trucks up on tram there until morning.	
	do	9 p.m.	Orders received from A.D.M.S. to return to barn — completed & reported for duty. Waited at barn onwards.	
		12 p.m.	Rainy heavily. Gas shells falling in neighbourhood. Wounded being brought in.	
	28/8/17	3 a.m.	A.D.S. full of cases so sent out 4 transport to scene and ammunition train. Personnel distributed to assist in off loading ammunition. Rain ceased.	

Army Form C. 2118.

WAR DIARY
or
INTELLIGENCE SUMMARY

(Erase heading not required.)

OC 129 Field Ambulance

Place	Date	Hour	Summary of Events and Information	Remarks and references to Appendices
GALLWITZ	28/9/17	4-30 a.m	Evacuated 10 lying & 16 sitting cases on train. Three more taken away the YPRES - BOESINGHE ROAD. No more to CHEAPSIDE for army T evacuation. Bearer relies & continued throughout the journey.	
SOLFERINO	do	5-30 a.m	Arrived. Sent stretchers & blankets to GALLWITZ on empty truck. Sent for M.A.C. cars.	
		7am	Train arrived with 4 lying cases. 12 cases being dropped at CHEAPSIDE.	
		8.45	10 lying, 26 sitting cases sent from Gallwitz. Proceeded to ADS in train.	
GALLWITZ		9.10	16 lying + 6 sitting sent down in train	
		10-30	11 " 13 "	
		11-45	13 " 3 " Proceeded with the train	
SOLFERINO		12-15 p	Arrived. Bearers trip early closed.	
PELISSIER FARM		1 p.m.	Capt N Brown returned from duty with 10 EnTB.	
		4	Lieut J.S. Knight & Lieut J.B. Gee U.S. medical service joined for duty.	
		6 pm	ASmS & Padre arrived. Withdrew part of personnel from SOLFERINO.	

Army Form C. 2118.

WAR DIARY
or
INTELLIGENCE SUMMARY.

(Erase heading not required.)   O.C. /29 Fd Amb.

Instructions regarding War Diaries and Intelligence Summaries are contained in F. S. Regs., Part II. and the Staff Manual respectively. Title pages will be prepared in manuscript.

Place	Date	Hour	Summary of Events and Information	Remarks and references to Appendices
Att PELISSIER FARM	29/8/17		No further action so light railway not used to clear casualties. Blood donor'd WOLFERINO & withdrew magnet'd transp't from the CHEAPSIDE.	A/1
"	30/8/17		ADMS called. Capt Rev returned to R.Q. also Lieut Dunn.	A/2
"	31/8/17		Lieut Dunn proceeded on leave. April injured right arm & dislocated military medals distinguished service conferred to many of this unit. Lieut Dunn proceeded CHEAPSIDE Capt H.A. Barton proceed on duty with 131 F. Amb & other S.S. strength present. Two reinforcements arrived who were formerly with the unit.	A/3

Howe
Lieut-Colonel
O.C. 129 Field Ambulance

N.J. Hawkins Cpl
A.D.M.S. 3rd Division

129TH FIELD AMBULANCE

SECRET.

WAR DIARY. Vol. 19

129 FIELD AMBULANCE.

SEPTEMBER 1917.

ORIGINAL COPY.

COMMITTEE FOR THE
MEDICAL HISTORY OF THE WAR
Date 5 NOV. 1917

B.E.F.

SUMMARY OF MEDICAL WAR DIARIES FOR
129th F.A., 38th Div., 14th Corps, 5th Army.

WESTERN FRONT JUNE,-SEPT. 1917.

O.C. Lt. Col. W.B. Edwards.

SUMMARISED UNDER THE FOLLOWING HEADINGS.

Phase "D" 1 Passchendaele Operations July-Nov. 1917
(a) Operations commencing 1st July 1917.

Sept	5th.	<u>Casualties R.A.M.C.</u> Lt. A.G. Dunn killed.
		<u>Moves Detachment:</u> O and 21 for duty with 130th Field Ambulance on canal bank.
	11th.	<u>Moves:</u> -To Singapore Camp nr. Proven.
	14th.	<u>Moves and Transfer.</u> To Eecke area on transfer to 11th Corps 1st Army.

Sept 5th.   Casualties R.A.M.C. Lt. A.G. Dunn killed.

            Moves Detachment: O and 21 for duty with 130th Field
            Ambulance on canal bank.

     11th. Moves: To Singapore Camp nr. Proven.

     14th. Moves and Transfer. To Eecke area on transfer to
            11th Corps 1st Army.

WAR DIARY or INTELLIGENCE SUMMARY

Army Form C. 2118.
129th Field Ambulance

(Erase heading not required.) .O.C. 129. Field Ambulance

Place	Date	Hour	Summary of Events and Information	Remarks and references to Appendices
PELISSIER FARM nr ELVERDINGHE	1/9/17		Nothing to report. Affi: 48788 Sgt. Edwards reported from C.C.S. also 47051 L/Cpl Roby & 64155 Pte W Walker from Base depot	A/S
do	2/9/17		Capt W Browne proceeded for duty at Corps Adv Collecting Post vice Capt B.W. Revill who returned to H.Q. Nothing noted concerned with him.	A/S
do	3/9/17		Nothing to Report Office.	A/S
do	4/9/17		Proceeded for temporary duty at Div H.Q. vice Barons on leave. Capt F.F. Rue took over charge of unit.	A/S
do	5/9/17		Lieut A.G. DUNN RAMC proceeded for duty as MO i/c 10th W.Yks Regt & was killed in action same night. Lieut F.S. WRIGHT. MORC. USA proceeded for duty as MO i/c Dn Walking Wded Collecting Post CHEASPSIDE. Regt Cols - 90 O.R. proceeded for duty on Canal bank with 130th Fld Amb. Capt W.W. BROWNE RAMC proceeded for temporary duty with 92nd & 95th Heavy Artillery groups. Capt G.W RIDDEL RAMC relieved Capt BROWNE at 14th Corps Adv Collecting Post S a/s G.R. Category A to Turn proceeded to MT & Base depot LE HAVRE. Admis. visited out 2 noble granted leave 1 April & Base returned from leave.	97. Leave Captains

2449 Wt. W14957/M90 750,000 1/16 J.B.C. & A. Forms/C.2118/12.

WAR DIARY
or
INTELLIGENCE SUMMARY

(Erase heading not required.)

FIELD AMBULANCE

O.C 129 Fd Amb.

Instructions regarding War Diaries and Intelligence Summaries are contained in F. S. Regs., Part II. and the Staff Manual respectively. Title Pages will be prepared in manuscript.

Place	Date	Hour	Summary of Events and Information	Remarks and references to Appendices
PELISSIER FARM nr ELVERDINGHE	6/9/17		Advance Party of 60th Fd Amb. arrived at Pelissier Farm	ap/l
do	1/9/17		ADMS visited StOs & examined PB lines. 3 RAMC 7 ASC returned from leave Capt D.K. Parkes RAMC joined for duty	Apl
do	8/9/17		2 RAMC granted leave and 1 returned. 1 reinforcement joined	apl
do	9/9/17		Capt BROWNE rejoined Unit from 92nd & 85th Heavy Art. Grps. Holding Party returned from SOLFERINO Fm having handed over to 60th Fd Amb. CHARIOT (?) B wdrs. Coll. Pt. handed over to 61st Fd Amb. under new 1st Corps. Sick Coll. Pt. handed over to 61st Fd Amb. Bgd Hdqrs & HDR Proceeded on Advance Party to SINGAPORE Camp (PELISSIER Fm handed over to 60th Fd Amb) Sgt. F.S.WRIGHT M.R.C. USA Proceeded to duty as MO/c Div. Reinforcement Camp Sgt. J.B. GOLD MOPE USA proceeded on temporary duty with Sgm Dur NFC 480. 29 Sergt W.J. PARKER & RAMC Pr. & WILLIAMSON awarded Military Medal	apl

2449 Wt. W14957/Mgo 750,000 1/16 J.B.C. & A. Forms/C.2118/12.

WAR DIARY
or
INTELLIGENCE SUMMARY

(Erase heading not required.) O.C. 129 Fd Amb

Instructions regarding War Diaries and Intelligence Summaries are contained in F.S. Regs., Part II. and the Staff Manual respectively. Title Pages will be prepared in manuscript.

Place	Date	Hour	Summary of Events and Information	Remarks and references to Appendices
PELISSIER FM & ELVERDINGHE	18/9/17		Horse Transport left PELISSIER Fm at 6 o'clock am for SINGAPORE Camp. Unit marched off at 10.15 am & ELVERDINGHE entrained there for INTERNATIONAL CORNER & from there marched to SINGAPORE Camp. Lieut L.T. MARKHAM RAMC joined for duty. 2 Men granted leave and Pictures	Appx
SINGAPORE Camp Nr PROVEN	19/9/17		Padre visits camp. Sergt Major BOLLAND + 1 OR granted leave. 1 Nurse returned from leave. Lieut L.M. DICKSON rejoined from leave. Capt N. BROWNE RAMC proceeded to England en route for MESOPOTAMIA	22L
do	20/9/17		Advance Party 9 OR proceeded to ZEZOGES	22L
do	21/9/17		Advance Pk 1 NCO proceeded to A.D.S. at LA CROIX les CORNEX. O/C & Offrs attended conference at 113th Inf Brigade HQrs	22L
do	24/9/17		Advance Party 10 OR proceeded to H.Q.S. of LE NOUVEAU MONDE. Unit & transport marched to EECKE and into Brigade Column. 9 O.R. granted leave	22L.

WAR DIARY
or
INTELLIGENCE SUMMARY

(Erase heading not required.)

O.C. 129 Fd Amb

Instructions regarding War Diaries and Intelligence Summaries are contained in F.S. Regs., Part II. and the Staff Manual respectively. Title Pages will be prepared in manuscript.

Place	Date	Hour	Summary of Events and Information	Remarks and references to Appendices
ECLT OIS	13/9/17		Capt Croomfel granted leave. Unit & Transport reached with Brigade.	A
MORBECQUE area	14/9/17		Capt NODEL ROWE & 6 OR proceeded to take over Ambulance Pt at ZELOBES. Lieut DICKSON ARNE & 9 OR proceeded to take over Post at LE CROIX DE CORNET. Unit Transport marched with Brigade between ST ESTAIRE & from Hd Qrs Western Field Amb to LE NOUVEAU MONDE (taking over Ambulance Pt from 98 Wessex Field Amb). 57 F.S. Division. O/C reported Unit from Temporary duty as SDRAS H 88 16. Pte Gilbert rejoins unit. 54 C & B sent P.U.O.	M
LE NOUVEAU MONDE	17/9/17		A.D.M.S. XI Corps visited. Large amount of work required to put the site in a satisfactory condition. Capt Rice proceeded on finding time 7CO & 15 OR.	A
do	18/9/17		Posns - OC 130 Fd Amb inspected site. Capt EW Riddel promoted 14 Employed on Kennel Trenchard. Lund broken. Proceeded to ZELOBES for duty and Lieut Trenchard to ADMS. Sgt J M Jones returned from Base. Pte Price transferred to 130 Fd Amb.	A

WAR DIARY
or
INTELLIGENCE SUMMARY

(Erase heading not required.)

O.C. 129 Fd Amb

Instructions regarding War Diaries and Intelligence Summaries are contained in F. S. Regs., Part II. and the Staff Manual respectively. Title Pages will be prepared in manuscript.

Place	Date	Hour	Summary of Events and Information	Remarks and references to Appendices
NOUVEAU MONDE	19/9/17		Capt J H Barker reported from 16th RWF	AF
do	20/9/17		G.O.C. 38 Div & acting ADMS inspected site. Train ADS & dressing station at ZELOBES	AF
do	21/9/17		acting ADMS reports inspected site & afterwards proceeded to ADS and RAP.	AF
do	22/9/17		Visited ADS & ZELOBES	AF
do	23/9/17		Inspected nightlying transport lines	AF
do	24/9/17		Visited ADS & RAP. Capt W M BADENOCH joined for duty from England.	AF
do	25/9/17		ADMS XI Corps accompanied by acting ADMS & DADMS inspected site H 8040 Brig. Williams reported from base	AF
do	26/9/17		Demonstration by Emerling Surgeon 1st Army given on "Thomas's splint" at which Reg. Surgeon J. Firma, Shicks trainer were attended. Lieut J B Cole USA Reported from duty, not DAC	AF
do	27/9/17		Proceeded to ZELOBES & BRCS.	AF
do	28/9/17		Lieut L M Markham proceeded to take over medical charge 11th CWB3. Capt Badenoch proceeded to duty at ADS vice Lieut Markham	AF

WAR DIARY
or
INTELLIGENCE SUMMARY

(Erase heading not required.) O.C. 129 Fd Amb.

Place	Date	Hour	Summary of Events and Information	Remarks and references to Appendices
NOUVEAU MONDE	29/9/17		Capt J.J Rees returned from leave. North ZELOBES	
do	30/9/17		Annual inspection Ett. Proceeded on ten days leave.	

A.G. Thompson
Col.
A.D.M.S. 38th Div.

[signature]
Lieut Col.
O.C. 129 Fd Amb.

Original Copy
Vol 20

War Diary

129th Field Ambulance

OCTOBER 1917

Army Form C. 2118.

WAR DIARY
or
INTELLIGENCE SUMMARY
(Erase heading not required.)

129TH FIELD AMBULANCE O.C. 129 Fd Amb

Place	Date	Hour	Summary of Events and Information	Remarks and references to Appendices
LA NOUVEAU MONDE (G.9.16.6) (Sh.51.50)	1 Oct 1917		Captain J.H. BANKES RAMC visited railroad LA GORGUE & classified men of 1 Hampshire (Garrison) Batt. R.R. men employed there. 2 O.R. granted leave. 3 O.R. returned.	Appleo Captains
"	2nd		D.M.S. 1st Army accompanied by A.D.M.S. (30th Div) visited self. A.D.M.S. + D.A.D.M.S. returned & examined men for P.B. Li Name + 1 B.S.C. H.T. returned from leave	9M
"	3rd		O/c visited ZEGERS. 1 None proceeded on leave + 1 None + 1 A.S.C. H.T. returned	9M
"	4th		O/c visited M.S.P. Captain J.H. BANKES RAMC attended board of enquiry into death of a man of 1st Batt. thought to have committed suicide, held at ZEDRES. 2 Ranks returned from leave. Regimental canteen opened. All ranks put for inspection. I selected & became a good man.	9M
"	5th		Lieut. J.B. GOLD U.S. M.O.R.C. proceeded to relieve Capt. LATIMER RAMC as M.O./c 181 R.F.A. Capt F.T. ROSS RAMC attended A.D.M.S. conference of all M.O's in Division	9M

WAR DIARY
or
INTELLIGENCE SUMMARY

(Erase heading not required.)

Army Form C. 2118.

129TH FIELD AMBULANCE

O-Z 129

Instructions regarding War Diaries and Intelligence Summaries are contained in F. S. Regs., Part II. and the Staff Manual respectively. Title Pages will be prepared in manuscript.

Place	Date	Hour	Summary of Events and Information	Remarks and references to Appendices
LA NOUVRE MONDE	Sept 5/17		Captain QW RIDDEL RAMC returned from leave. 2 ORs NT + 1 RAMC returned from leave. 2ORs MT granted leave	GW
	6"		O/C visited ZELOBES	GW
	7"		Watches put back one hour at 1AM 3 RAMC + 1 ASC NT returned from leave	GW
	8"		O/C accompanied MONS & TOS + hg'ters O/Post	GW
	9"		ADMS visited Off + examined men for 78 + T.U. + afterwards proceeded to ZELOBES ft Same purpose. Lieut Dickson RAMC proceeded to duty with 130" Field Ambulance 5 OR men reported for duty to replace 5 ARC NT Category A' men. Captain AW RIDDEL proceeded + ZELOBES for duty.	GW
	10.		1 RAMC granted leave	GW
	11"		3 RAMC returned from leave 3 RAMC granted leave.	GW

WAR DIARY
or
INTELLIGENCE SUMMARY

(Erase heading not required.)   O.C. 129 Fd Amb.

Army Form C. 2118.

129TH FIELD AMBULANCE

Place	Date	Hour	Summary of Events and Information	Remarks and references to Appendices
LA NOUVEAU MONDE	11th Oct 1917	5 A.M	Category "A" proceeded to report to MT&S Base Depot HAVRE.	AM
do	12		Lieut Colonel A. JONES R.A.M.C. rejoined from leave.	AM
			2/Lieut C. GRANTED R.A.M.C Joined unit	AM
			A.D.M.S inspected billets	AM
do	13		D.A.D.M.S visited the unit	AM
do	14		480111 Pte J. Williams wounded to C.C.S.	AM
			inspected A.M.S.	
do	15		Mobile ambulance arrived at ZELOBES.	
			Capt J.A. Baker proceeded to LA FORGUE to classify men of 42nd Garrison H'Qrs Batn with a view to transfer to labour Coy	AM
			A.D.M.S visited water site	
			1734 Sgt W Dixon joined for duty.	
			Lieut 2nd J Maxby proceeded on ten days leave	
do	16		Capt T.J. Ress proceeded to ZELOBES for duty and Capt O W Rowell returned to R.Q.	AM
			A.A+2 m.s + D.A.D 38 Div. inspected Ambulance site.	
			A.D.M.S visited inspected men found to be unfit for duty in the forward area	

WAR DIARY
or
INTELLIGENCE SUMMARY

(Erase heading not required.) O.C. 129 Fd Amb.

Army Form C. 2118.

129TH FIELD AMBULANCE

Instructions regarding War Diaries and Intelligence Summaries are contained in F. S. Regs., Part II. and the Staff Manual respectively. Title Pages will be prepared in manuscript.

Place	Date	Hour	Summary of Events and Information	Remarks and references to Appendices
LE NOUVEAU MONDE (LA GORGE)	17/6/17		ADMS XI Corps inspected site also RSMO. Attended conference of officers commanding medical units at ADMS Office	AS
do	18/6/17		Visited AAA P.R.A.P.	AS
do	19/6/17		Visited ZELOBES	AS
do	20/6/17		Visited A.D.S. ADMS inspected horse lines	AS
do	21/6/17		Capt W. Badcock proceeded for duty with 10th Bath Welch Regt. Sgt J.R. Benders proceeded for duty to A.D.S. Lieut J.B. Gye A.S.R. returned from duty with 121 By R.F.A.	AS
do	22/6/17		ADMS inspected inspection site and afterwards inspected personnel & kit and 2nd kit were inspected.	AS
do	23/6/17		ADMS visited & inspected numerous food stuff to be useful for duty in trans'sit area inspected maxx of personal. Proceeded to ZELOBES with ADMS inspected site & decided to carry out various structural improvement.	AS
do	24/6/17		Advance party sent to ZELOBES to carry out improvements for ADMS XI Corps intended that material would be supplied by X Corps	AS

WAR DIARY
or
INTELLIGENCE SUMMARY

Army Form C. 2118.

(Erase heading not required.) O.C. 129 Fd Amb

Place	Date	Hour	Summary of Events and Information	Remarks and references to Appendices
LE NOUVEAU MONDE (LA GORGUE)	25/10/17		Lieut J.B. Grth M.O. proceeded to temporary duty with 14 Bath Rn F. Posted R.E. party to obtain material. Proceeded ANS & RAP at EATON HALL & afterwards went round the support line of the sector clearing the Fd Amb.	A.J.
do	26/10/17		Visited Hd Ml office	A.J.
do	27/10/17		Cpl R.E. Miller joined for duty from 131 Fd Amb. A.M.S. Bath & Water. 1st Bn't Band played during the afternoon in the hospital grounds	A.J. A.J.
do	28/10/17		Inspected cook at ZELOBES.	A.J.
do	29/10/17		Lt J. Mc. Varley returned from leave. Capt McMullan proceeded to LA GORGUE to examine R.B. men at Rablant	A.J.
do	30/10/17		Capt Cook & a Lynndine from 2 Wd Gre attended demonstration in baking at Army Sch. A.D.M.S. examined unfit men. Proceeded to ZELOBES with A.D.M.S. All personnel inspected & classified – A, those fit for transfer to Infantry, + B those unfit	A.J. A.J.
do	31/10/17		Proceeded A.D.S. & afternoon to CONVENT AVENUE RAP & FORDY FARM Proceed to ARMENTIERS with D.M.S. Capt Riddell proceeded to ZELOBES /a..m./ Cpl Rees returned from ZELOBES	A.J.

A.G. Thompson
A.D.M.S.

Howard Knowl Col
O.C. 129 Fd Ambulance
38 (Welsh) Div.

Original Copy

129 Field Ambulance

War Diary.

NOVEMBER 1917

COMMITTEE FOR THE
MEDICAL HISTORY OF THE WAR
Date 17 JAN. 1918

Army Form C. 2118.

WAR DIARY
or
INTELLIGENCE SUMMARY

(Erase heading not required.) Of 129 Ft Amber

129TH FIELD AMBULANCE.

Instructions regarding War Diaries and Intelligence Summaries are contained in F. S. Regs., Part II. and the Staff Manual respectively. Title Pages will be prepared in manuscript.

Place	Date	Hour	Summary of Events and Information	Remarks and references to Appendices
LE NOUVEAU MONDE (LA GORGE)	1/11/17		Capt G.W. Riddel proceeded to ZELOBES for duty, Capt F.J. Rees returning to HQ on relief. Capt G.N. Loveman M.C. and Capt J.V. Somerville M.C. joined for duty	A.F
do	2/11/17		ADMS XI Corps, ADMS & DADMS 38 Div. inspected hospital auto & afterwards proceeded to 39 D.S.	A.F
do	3/11/17		Attended conference of M.O.'s at 131 Ft Amb accompanied by Captains Rees, Loveman, Somerville. Capt. R.G. McMillan took over charge of ADS.	A.F
do	4/11/17		Capt J.H. Banks, Capt.Comdg 38 Div. inspected the Ambulance Car Reinforcement by the A.D.M.S.	A.F
do	5/11/17		Brig-Gen C.W. ALEXANDER V.C. Temp Commandg 38 Div. inspected the A.D.S. & 2 m.b. Capt G.N. Loveman M.C. proceeded for personal duty with 14th Bath R.W.F. in relief of Reid F.S. Capt U.S.R. into reported this unit.	A.F
do	6/11/17		ADMS mobilized, inspected new reported beautiful for duty in the forward area. Capt J.H. Banks & Capt Major Bolland attended demonstration on the "Anti-lines" at 113 Bde H.Q.	A.F
do	7/11/17		Capt J.V. Somerville proceeded for temporary duty with 13th Bath Welsh Regt.	A.F
do	8/11/17		A.D.O.S 38 Div. visited the A.D.S. & inspected stores & equipment. Capt J.H. Banks proceeded on 14 days leave. Visited Reechan at ZELOBES. DADMS called	A.F
do	9/11/17		48783 Pte Davis transferred to 33 Labour Group for duty as medical orderly with 67 Chinese Labour Compy.	A.F
do	10/11/17		Visited ADS & Reg Aid Posts	A.F
do	11/11/17		ADMS DADMS called. Capt Rees proceeded to LA GORGE Railhead to inspect P.B. men due for transfer to Employment Coy	A.F

Army Form C. 2118.

WAR DIARY
or
INTELLIGENCE SUMMARY

(Erase heading not required.) O.C. 129 F. Amb.

Instructions regarding War Diaries and Intelligence Summaries are contained in F. S. Regs., Part II. and the Staff Manual respectively. Title Pages will be prepared in manuscript.

129TH FIELD AMBULANCE.

Place	Date	Hour	Summary of Events and Information	Remarks and references to Appendices
LE NOUVEAU MONDE (LA GORGE)	13/11/17		ADMS inspected men reported to be unfit for duty in forward area. ADMS passed ambulance	AJ
	14/11/17		Capt S.W. Riddell, 48773 Sgt W. Runci & 48761 Cpl W. Brown proceeded to attend a course of instruction at the First Army R.A.M.C. School. Capt Reco proceeded to ZELOBES for duty.	AJ
do	16/11/17		Herbert Henderson ZELOBES	AJ
do	17/11/17		ADMS inspected site	AJ
do	18/11/17		Noted RSG & RAP's	AJ
do	20/11/17		ADMS inspected men reported to be unfit for duty in the forward area. Inspected personnel in full marching order.	AJ
do	21/11/17		S.S.O called with reference to supply of coal & paraffin	AJ
do	22/11/17		Capt Somerville returned from duty with 1/3 Batt Welsh Regt	AJ
do	23/11/17		Capt Banks returned from leave	AJ
do	24/11/17		Capt Somerville proceeded for duty with 2nd Division. Lieut C.B. Wood W.S.R. joined for duty from 2nd Division. Capt Riddell & 2 NCO's returned to ZELOBES from First Army R.A.M.B. school. Capt Reco returned to HQ from ZELOBES.	AJ
do	25/11/17		Colonel Dunn - acting ADMS XV Corps inspected Ambulance site accompanied by ADMS 38 Div. 38 DN	AJ
do	26/11/17		Capt Reco proceeded to ZA GORGE Railhead to inspect P.B men due for transfer to Employment Coy	AJ
do	27/11/17		ADMS inspected men reported to be unfit for duty in the forward area.	AJ
do	28/11/17		Acting ADMS XV Corps DADMS XV Corps inspected site. DA & QMG 38 Div accompanied by a Staff Officer of XV Corps inspected site	AJ

Army Form C. 2118.

WAR DIARY
or
INTELLIGENCE SUMMARY

(Erase heading not required.) O C 129 Fd Amb

129th FIELD AMBULANCE

Instructions regarding War Diaries and Intelligence Summaries are contained in F. S. Regs., Part II. and the Staff Manual respectively. Title Pages will be prepared in manuscript.

Place	Date	Hour	Summary of Events and Information	Remarks and references to Appendices
LE NOUVEAU MONDE (LA GORGUE)	28/11/17		Capt McMillan proceeded temporary duty unit 131 Bde R.F.A. Lieut Wood U.S.R. proceeded to A.D.S. for duty.	
do	29/11/17		1 Sergt. proceeded to First Army School for corresp. instruction. A.A. & Q.M.G. 38 Div & D.A. & Q.M.G. XV Corps inspected site.	
do	30/11/17		A.D.M.S. inspected marquette. Brit. Band played Hindoo & Jahuto in afternoon.	

A.G. Thompson Col.
A.D.M.S. 38th Div.

Manuel
Lieut. Col.
R.A.M.C.
O.C. 129 Fd Amb

WAR DIARY.

129 FIELD AMBULANCE

DECEMBER 1917.

ORIGINAL COPY.

WAR DIARY
or
INTELLIGENCE SUMMARY

(Erase heading not required.) O.C. 129 F.A. Amb[?]

Army Form C. 2118.

129TH FIELD AMBULANCE

Instructions regarding War Diaries and Intelligence Summaries are contained in F.S. Regs., Part II. and the Staff Manual respectively. Title Pages will be prepared in manuscript.

Place	Date	Hour	Summary of Events and Information	Remarks and references to Appendices
LE NOUVEAU MONDE (LA GORGUE)	1/12/17		Visited A.D.S. & R.A.P.	A/J
	2/12/17		Visited ZELOBES	A/J
	3/12/17		G.O.C. 38th Div. inspected the Amb.	A/J
	4/12/17		ADMS XV Corps inspected site & afterwards proceeded to A.D.S.	A/J
do	5/12/17		DADMS XV Corps accompanied by DAQMG XV Corps inspected site	A/J
do	6/12/17		GOC XV Corps proceeded to BOIS GRENIER A.D.S.	A/J
do	7/12/17		Capt Rowe proceeded to ZELOBES for duty vice Capt Roddil who proceeded to BOIS GRENIER A.D.S.	A/J
do	8/12/17		Took over A.D.S. at BOIS GRENIER from 130 Fd Amb. Capt McMillan returned from 121 Bde R.F.A.	A/J
			ADMS 29th ADMS inspected site	
do	10/12/17		Patrecued [?] ADS at LE CROIX LES CORNEX & handed it over to 2nd NZ C.C.R.	A/J
			Visiting ZELOBES ADMS inspected	
do	11/12/17		ADMS inspected hosp. now & afterwards proceeded to ZELOBES	A/J
do	15/12/17		G.O.C. 38 Div. inspected site. ADMS called. Lieut Col MARCY MO proceeded to duty	A/J
			from 29 M Armsen [?]	
			DDMS XV Corps inspected site	
do	16/12/17			A/J
do	17/12/17		Capt McMillan reverted for duty with 16th Batt (Welsh) Regt	A/J
do	18/12/17		Capt C Kelly M.C. joining for duty	A/J
do	19/12/17		Capt C Kelly M.C. proceeded for duty with 130 Fd Amb. Lieut F Cameron proceeded for duty from 130 Fd Amb	A/J
			Lieut E B Wood M.S. M.O RC proceeded to ADS at LE CROIX LES CORNEX to take over from 2nd Bat NZ C.C.P.	A/J

WAR DIARY
or
INTELLIGENCE SUMMARY

(Erase heading not required.) O.C. 129 Fd Amb

Army Form C. 2118.

Instructions regarding War Diaries and Intelligence Summaries are contained in F. S. Regs., Part II. and the Staff Manual respectively. Title Pages will be prepared in manuscript.

Place	Date	Hour	Summary of Events and Information	Remarks and references to Appendices
LE NOUVEAU MONDE	20/12/17		A.D.S at BOIS GRENIER handed over to 131 Fd Amb, Capt Riddell + personnel returning to MDS	
(LA GORGUE)	21/12/17		This unit responsible for working up FLEURBAIX sector. Moved A.D.S. at LECROIX LES CORNEX and R.A.P at EATON HALL. Site at ZELOBES handed over to 130 Fd Amb	
do	22/12/17		AR-2M & 38 Dn. inoculated. 67477 Pte G. Whitfield, 32496 Pte Turner evacuated sick. - Wounded 48244 Pte A.G Reid, 48035 Pte W.J Davis admitted to hospital wounded	
do	23/12/17		Aprils usual late	
do	24/12/17		Opened the Red Cross on this site. Worten A.D.S	
do	25/12/17		Aprils inspected useful new. Worten A.D.S	
do	26/12/17		Capt Riddell attended lecture on War Savings at DW HQ. Lieut Macey proceeded to temporary duty with 13th Bn. btn half Bn. Lieut Gold adjoined Lieut Loyd at R.R.P. Proceeded to 79515 work. Assists + worner formed there + after evacing out posts	
do	27/12/17		H.Q.C 38 Dn. accompanied by an Ammunition General + Staff Officers inspected site	
do	28/12/17		Worten N.D.F.	
do	30/12/17		A.R & M.G XV. Corps inoculated.	
do	31/12/17		Party of RE's from Corps attached to each additional hut on the site	

A. Nuss Limbel
O.C 129 Fd Amb

WA 23
36

War Diary.
129th Field Ambulance
January 1918.

Original Copy

Army Form C. 2118.

WAR DIARY
or
INTELLIGENCE SUMMARY

(Erase heading not required.) O.C 129 Fd Ambulance

Instructions regarding War Diaries and Intelligence Summaries are contained in F. S. Regs., Part II. and the Staff Manual respectively. Title Pages will be prepared in manuscript.

Place	Date	Hour	Summary of Events and Information	Remarks and references to Appendices
LE NOUVEAU MONDE (LA GORGE)	1/1/18		Acting ADMS inspected sickful men. Lieut Cannon proceeded to ADS for duty - relieving Lieut Gold	
	2/1/18		Lieut Gold proceeded to temporary duty with 15th Bath W.R Regt.	
do	3/1/18		Worked ADS	
"	8/1/18		Acting ADMS inspected sickful men.	
"	9/1/18		Capt Riddel proceeded to ADS for duty vice Lieut Cannon who proceeded to First Army RAMC school. Lieut Biffin Morris rejoined from 13th Welsh Regt.	
"	10/1/18		DADMS XII Div. inspected site. Lieut Vachs administration H.Q. in B.company	
			Proceeded to VIEUX BERGUIN to inspect area	
"	11/1/18		O.C 37 Fd Amb. inspected site.	
			Returned vice On 13th.	
	12/1/18		ADS at LA CROIX LES CORNEX handed over to party from 36 Fd Amb. Capt Riddel returned to H.Q. Advance party sent to VIEUX BERQUIN. An advance party from 37 Fd Amb arrived to take over MDS. Lieut B/S. Wood U.S.M.O.R.C. wore sick to 54 CCS.	
	13/1/18	9 am	Handed over dinning station at LE NOUVEAU MONDE to No 37 Fd Amb.	
VIEUX BERGUIN		12 mn	Unit & transport arrived at VIEUX BERGUIN - taking over the billets occupied by 37 Fd Amb. Capt Riddel followed 114 Inf Bde with Horse Ambulance. very few Infantry field for on march.	
"	15/1/18		Capt Riddel proceeded Staff Captain 114 Bde to St HILAIRE AREA to inspect billets etc - reported that no suitable site for the accommodation of sick in that area. Lieut Morris proceeded to First Army RAMC school to attend Course in Sanitation etc. ADMS inspected sickful men.	

2449 Wt. W14957/Mgo 750,000 1/16 J.B.C. & A. Forms/C.2118/12.

WAR DIARY
or
INTELLIGENCE SUMMARY

Army Form C. 2118.

(Erase heading not required.) O.C. 129 Fd Amb.

Place	Date	Hour	Summary of Events and Information	Remarks and references to Appendices
VIEUX BERQUIN	16/1/18		Visited A.D.M.S. Office afterwards proceeded to NORRENT FONTES to select out for Ambulance	
Same	18/1/18		4 NCO's + 2 Ptes proceeded on advance party to QUARBECQUE. Assumed Temporary Command of unit.	P.S. Coo
QUARBECQUE	19/1/18		Lieut Col A. JONES MC RAMC granted special leave (1 month) to United Kingdom Unit + transport marched to QUARBECQUE. Lieut J B GOLD V.C. MORC promoted to Captain as from 19/1/18. Capt J.S. GOLD V.C MORC returned from temporary duty with 14 F.Amb. Lieut C.H. MARCY V.C. RAMC + Lieut F. CAMERON RAMC + 1 NCO reported from Course at 1st Army school of Instruction. Advance Party 4 O.R. proceeded to NORRENT FONTES.	PM1
NORRENT FONTES	20/1/18		Unit transport marched to NORRENT FONTES. Ambulance car detailed to duty with 122 Bde R.F.A. + Allies Bde + two lorries on the march to remain with item during period of training. Lieut CAMERON RAMC proceeded for duty to 10th Bn Welsh Regt.	W.R
	22/1/18		# 1 RAMC O.R. granted leave	W.1

2449 Wt. W14957/Mg0 750,000 1/16 J.B.C. & A. Forms/C.2118/12.

Army Form C. 2118.

WAR DIARY
or
INTELLIGENCE SUMMARY.
(Erase heading not required.)

Place	Date	Hour	Summary of Events and Information	Remarks and references to Appendices
Same	23/1/18		Capt J.B. GOID DC MOPC + 2 NCO's proceeded to attend course at 1st Army School of Instruction	OM
	26/1/18		ADMS visited sick + inspected unit's men	OM
	28/1/18	10.0 AM	F. 14th Bn Attack Regt admitted accidentally wounded during training	OM
		11.15	RIFLE	
			Long Service + Good Conduct medal awarded to T/14057 2 S.S.M EVANS. B ASC. HT	

J.D. MAY
Capt. R.A.M.C.
i/c 129 Field Ambulance

W.G. Thompson
ADMS C Col
38th Div.

War Diary.

129 Field Ambulance.

February 1918.

COMMITTEE FOR THE
MEDICAL HISTORY OF THE WAR
Date 8 APR 1918

Original Copy

WAR DIARY
or
INTELLIGENCE SUMMARY.

(Erase heading not required.)

Army Form C. 2118.

129TH FIELD AMBULANCE

Place	Date	Hour	Summary of Events and Information	Remarks and references to Appendices
NORRENT FONTES	1/2/18		113 Inf Bgde relieved 114 Inf Bgde in ST HILAIRE AREA. Horse Ambulance accompanied Battalion on the march.	2nd Lieut. Capt More
"	2/2/18		ADMS visited A.D.S. + inspected men unfit for the forward area. ADMS presented the ribbon of the Long Service & Good Conduct medal to S.S.M. EVANS. B A.S.C. A.T. Capt GOULD MORC. DN Cpt returned from 1st Army School.	ADM
	3/2/18		Accompanied by Lt QM J VARLEY RAMC the O/C investigated area West of STEENWERCK with a view to finding site suitable for Main Dressing Station in the event of active operations. 1/Lt Cpt MABEY MORC USA proceeded to take over temporary medical charge of 30th S.F.C. "Franks" (the unit dental [part 5] performed at the Canadian School of Instruction & Reinforcement camp at LIERES.	ADM
	7/2/18		Association Football Competition. 3rd Round. Won.	ADM

WAR DIARY
or
INTELLIGENCE SUMMARY.
(Erase heading not required.)

Army Form C. 2118.

129TH FIELD AMBULANCE.

Place	Date	Hour	Summary of Events and Information	Remarks and references to Appendices
NORRENT FONTES	9/9/18		1st H.V. HANSON US MORE } Joined for duty 1/Lt E.L. PATTERSON US MORE } ADMS visited pits & inspected new unit for forward area	poke
	10/9/18		O/c presented ribbon of Mons Star to 12 NCO+ men on parade. 48826 Pte EDWARDS T. awarded Belgian Croix de Guerre.	M
	11/9/18		O/c attended conference of O/c Ambulances at ADMS' Office.	M.
	12/9/18		113th Inf Bgde Sports. - O/c adjudicated in Ambulance Competition for Batt. Stretcher bearers awarded the prize to Transfrs from 1/5 R.W.F.	M
	13/9/18		Advance Party of 2 NCOT + 2 OR proceeded to GUARBECQUE at 9am & took over billet. Unit personnel & Transport marched to GUARBECQUE. NCO + LUR proceeded on Advance Party to STEENBECK.	M.

WAR DIARY
or
INTELLIGENCE SUMMARY.
(Erase heading not required.)

Army Form C. 2118.

129TH FIELD AMBULANCE.

Place	Date	Hour	Summary of Events and Information	Remarks and references to Appendices
GURBECQUE	14/7/18		Advance Party - Capt G.W. RIDDEL RAMC, 1 N.C.O, 12 O.R. proceeded to NEUF BERQUIN. Unit - Ground Transport - marched to NEUF BERQUIN.	Poster
NEUF BERQUIN	15/7/18		Unit marched to STEENWERCK. F. AMBCE.	ord
STEENWERCK	16/7/18		Handed over charge to Capt G.W. RIDDEL R.A.M.C. & proceeded to take over Temporary Command of 131st Field Amb vice Lt Col Rt Hon. M.r C. ROBERTS to 41 Stationary Hospital.	2/Lieut Capt R.A.M.C.
Same	16/7/18		Assumed charge of unit. June O.R. proceeded as orderly to Trench foot centre at Robelarie. Twenage, Port de Nieppe, Square Farm and Longrighem Laundry. A.D.M.S. visited site.	Stonesield
Same	17/7/18		Attended lecture on "German Gas Appliances" at XV Corps Gas School. Lt. Patterson, E.B. U.S.M.O.R.C. proceeded to take over medical charge of 15th Welsh Regiment his struck off strength of unit. Capt. Friel R.A.M.C. joined for duty from 15th Welsh Regiment to take on strength of unit. G.O.C. Division inspected site. One N.C.O. granted leave.	8152

Army Form C. 2118.

WAR DIARY
or
INTELLIGENCE SUMMARY.
(Erase heading not required.)

[19th FIELD AMBULANCE]

Instructions regarding War Diaries and Intelligence Summaries are contained in F. S. Regs., Part II. and the Staff Manual respectively. Title pages will be prepared in manuscript.

Place	Date	Hour	Summary of Events and Information	Remarks and references to Appendices
STEENWERCK	18/7/18		Six O.R. of 235th Employment Company attached to unit proceeded to 49th Sanitary Section for duty. Lt. Col. Jones M.C. R.A.M.C. returned from leave.	Steenwerck [Paper Names]
"	19/7/18		Visited ADMS Office & afterwards proceeded to WATERLANDS CAMP and LA BLANCHE MAISON with a view to ascertaining their suitability for Ambulance uses.	Home
"	20/7/18		Lieut Hanson & 3 NCO's proceeded to 2nd Army School of Instruction. Everetine with ADMS at LA BLANCHE MAISON	—
"	21/7/18		Attended Conference of medical Officers at 131 F. Amb.	—
"	22/7/18		Inspected unfit men with medical Board. Proceeded to LE VERRIER and LA BECQUE to see if there was suitable sites for a F. Amb. A number of farms used at LE VERRIER – they are good cover for wounded; tolerable accommodation for Officers, & lacking in accommodation or equipment etc – the filled farms formerly billets have it's accommodation troops for very shell friends. The situation of LE VERRIER is good as regards traffic routes – RE roads being in fair order & on the probable route forward in of [advance] of Lund C of Army. Reports from day with 38 D.S.6	—
"	23/7/18		Visited LE VERRIER with 2nd Lt [ ] to investigate more minutely the accommodation etc	—

WAR DIARY
or
INTELLIGENCE SUMMARY.

Army Form C. 2118.

FIELD AMBULANCE.

Place	Date	Hour	Summary of Events and Information	Remarks and references to Appendices
STEENWERCK	10/1/18		Capt. R.B. GITH & Lieut CATNACH proceeded 14 days leave to PARIS. Notes LE VERRIER nom ADT/S & assumed the various billets etc.	AJ
	1/2/18		Capt. Ruo returned from duty with 131 Infantry	AJ
	28/2/18		Capt Ruo proceeded on 14 days leave to ENGLAND. Capt Snell proceeded to CLARQUES for temporary duty with 41 Sanitary Sectn. Ground not same + AA DMS to LE VERRIER to select adj/w near Olousy.	AJ

J Thompson Col. DS.
ADMS 35th Div.

[signature]
Lieut Col RAMC
OC 129 Fd Amb.

"Secret"

WAR DIARY

Inclosing D/A

129th Field Ambulance

March 1918

Original Copy

Vol 25

Army Form C. 2118.

WAR DIARY
or
INTELLIGENCE SUMMARY.
(Erase heading not required.) O.C. 129 Fd Amb.

Instructions regarding War Diaries and Intelligence Summaries are contained in F.S. Regs., Part II. and the Staff Manual respectively. Title pages will be prepared in manuscript.

Place	Date	Hour	Summary of Events and Information	Remarks and references to Appendices
STEENWERCK	1/3/18		ADMS inspected useful men.	A
"	2/3/18		Proceeded to LE VERRIER with Claims Officer to obtain land for horse standings. Forwarded report to ADMS on suitability of LA BLANCHE MAISON & LE VERRIER as sites for the purpose.	A
"	3/3/18		Lieut H.J. Anson returned from 1st Army School.	A
"	4/3/18		Proceeded to LE VERRIER to inspect the piece of land offered by the farmer for horse standings & found quite suitable for that purpose.	A
"	5/3/18		Visited LE VERRIER with Adjutant R.E. to select another site for standings. At 2 P.M. a member of the sub-commission to give permission to occupy a piece of land which had been previously used by troops. Capt E.W. Rudd proceeded on Sunday special leave.	A
"	6/3/18		Visited LE VERRIER with 2nd in command Billets – afterwards arranged with Claims Officer for the occupation of the land for horse standings.	A
"	7/3/18		G.O.C. 38th Div. ADMS accompanied by the undermentioned members of the Corporation of Cardiff inspected the site :– Lt. Col A.H. Bird Deputy Ld. Hy. Sir Robert Lord Mayor. Hy. Sir Courtry J.P. Councillor Kirk J.P. Councillor Owen J.P.	A
"	8/3/18		Patients inspected useful men. Proceeded to LE VERRIER and ADMS IV Corps – arranged time round LE VERRIER & LA BLANCHE MAISON.	A
"	9/3/18		Summer formation. 6 reinforcements joined. Lieut Annon proceeded for duty with 10 Sents. Lieut Fuller Mourl taken on strength.	A

WAR DIARY
or
INTELLIGENCE SUMMARY.

(Erase heading not required.)

Army Form C. 2118.

O.C. 129 F. Amb.

Place	Date	Hour	Summary of Events and Information	Remarks and references to Appendices
STEENWERCK	10 March/18		Suffering from influenza & visited cholera engine at 54 C.C.S. Read 2nd duty proceeded 3.30 pm	AB
"	11		Evacuated to 54 C.C.S. — handed over to Bn. J.N. Banks	AB
"	12		To Le Verrier with A.D.M.S. + D.A.D.M.S. to see work starting	AB
"	13		Capt. J.B. Gold U.S.M.O.R.C. & 1/Lt. C.H. Macey rejoined unit from Paris leave. To Le Verrier with Adj. R.E. re material for side catchup	AB
"	15		1/Lieut. C.H. Macey U.S.M.O.R.C. detailed 9 July to A.D.M.S. 57th Division (temporary). A.D.M.S. examined R.S. men & inspected Steen werck site.	AB AB
"	16		Capt. Rees rejoined unit from 14 days leave. Visited Le Verrier	
"	17		O.C. rejoined unit from 12th Stationary Hospital. Received Command of unit. Lieut. Fowler proceeded 147 Bde R.F.A. for duty	
"	18		Visited A.D.M.S. rafflemans proceeded to LE VERRIER. Tul. Rnd. Officer there & arranged to requisition agreed Farm land to hospital site.	
"	19		Some shells shelling of the neighbourhood the evening.	
"	20		Unit moved to LE VERRIER — no officers & sufficient personnel remaining at STEENWERK — also the principal.	
LE VERRIER	21		Reported moved to LE VERRIER.	
"	22		Commenced work at new site & continued the construction of standing April & during called	

Army Form C. 2118.

WAR DIARY
or
INTELLIGENCE SUMMARY.
(Erase heading not required.) O.C. 129 Fd Amb.

Instructions regarding War Diaries and Intelligence Summaries are contained in F. S. Regs., Part II. and the Staff Manual respectively. Title pages will be prepared in manuscript.

Place	Date	Hour	Summary of Events and Information	Remarks and references to Appendices
LE VERRIER	24 hund		Lieut D.M. Vally strunk Honorary Rank of Captain	
"			Capt E.W. Reid to E acting major Whilst in command of Section from 4/4/18	
"	26		Lieut Mary regimed from 57 Div Party sent to STEENBECQUE to make fort for mercing pounts of 34 Div	
"	27		Rome work called	
"	28		Order received to report at Steenwerch 29 "	
"	29		Duty tractor arms officer arriving Sthna STEENWERCK Railhead. O.C. 103rd Fd Amb — Capt Field —	
"			from returning Fd A.O. O.C. 103rd Fd Amb called to see about arrangements	
"	30		Handed over billets etc. to 103 Fd Amb & moved to DOULIEU AREA.	
"			Attached to 114 Bde for the time — Capt Brooks doing Bde & made the necessary arrangements for billets etc. Rained heavily.	
DOULIEU AREA	31		Capt Reid made 114 Bde S.O. for orders as to move.	

W.S. Thornton
Col - comg 13-
Aun E.

Morris Bt.
Lieut Col.
O.C. 129 Fd Amb

YA 26

140/2900

COMMITTEE FOR THE
MEDICAL HISTORY OF THE WAR
Date — 6 JUN 1918

WAR DIARY
129 Field Ambulance
April 1915.

Original Copy

WAR DIARY or **INTELLIGENCE SUMMARY**
(Erase heading not required.)

Army Form C. 2118.

129TH FIELD AMBULANCE. O.C. 129 Fd Amb

Place	Date	Hour	Summary of Events and Information	Remarks and references to Appendices
DOULIEU	1/4/18	2 p.m.	Capt J.W. Banks proceeded to 131 Fd Amb for duty	
		7 p.m.	Horse transport moved off to MERVILLE in charge of Capt J.B. Gold	
		7.45 p.m.	Remainder of unit proceeded by motor ambulances to MERVILLE – Motor ambulances proceeding beyond to DOULLENS area.	
MERVILLE	2/4/18	1 a.m.	Unit entrained	
MONDECOURT	"	2 p.m.	Dis-entrained MONDECOURT. Proceeded to PAS & halted there for dinner – subsequently marching to HERISSART. Orders received on the route that 113 Bde moving to FORCEVILLE & that this unit was to proceed there. Proceeded to A.D.M.S. office & arranged to go to HERISSART. Notified Bde accordingly.	
HERISSART	"	9-30 p.m.	Unit arrived	
	3/4/18		Visited A.D.M.S. office. 113 Bde moved to TOUTENCOURT – HERISSART AREA	
	4/4/18		Conference at A.D.M.S. office	
	5/4/18		113 Bde moved to VADENCOURT – Four cars detained with them to collect cases regularly immediately. 114 Bde moved to HERISSART.	
	6/4/18		Made reconnaissance with Major Rees of the route etc. between BAISEUX and HENENCOURT. Made a reconnaissance also for bus posts etc. Reported to A.D.M.S. office. Received orders at 4 p.m. to move to RUBEMPRE at 5 p.m. Major Rees proceeded with an advance party to 113 Bde.	
RUBEMPRE	"	6-30 p.m.	Arrived at RUBEMPRE	
"	7/4/18		A.D.M.S. called. Cars inspected. Hutchridge. Lieut D.W. Bollands reported from leave.	

WAR DIARY
or
INTELLIGENCE SUMMARY.
(Erase heading not required.)

O.C. 129 Fd Amb.

Army Form C. 2118.

129TH FIELD AMBULANCE

Place	Date	Hour	Summary of Events and Information	Remarks and references to Appendices
RUDEMPRE	8/4/18		Major Ridel reported from leave. 48811 Pte J. Thomas sent to CCS with P.U.O.	AF
"	9/4/18		48686 Pte P. Micklewright was today suffering from P.U.O.	AF
			Capt R.S. de Cruey Bennett a/c to joined for duty. Capt J. Friel R.A.M.C. O/c 41 San. Sect. struck off strength.	
"	10/4/18		Proceeded with Major Ridel & 4 Amer N.C.O's to reconnoitre BAISEUX – FORCEVILLE line from V 3 c 2 0 to Corps Southern Boundary. Major Ridel & Lieut Morey also made a reconnaissance of Rio line. Capt A.S. Campbell joined for duty.	AF
			Proceeded with Major Ridel to CONTAY & interviewed A.D.M.S. 12 Div. re taking over the line & afterwards went on to WARLOY to obtain details of advance from O.C. 38 Fd Amb.	AF
"	11/4/18		Major Ridel, Lieut Morey & advance party proceeded to WARLOY to take over forward posts. Proceeded to WARLOY to arrange details of relief & then proceeded to MILLENCOURT. Called at 114th Bde H.Q. at HENENCOURT & Laby at A.D.M.S. Office. Major Ridel & advance party proceeded to MILLENCOURT to take over A.D.S. & Bearer Posts. Main body moved off at 1-30 p.m. – Arriving at WARLOY at 4 p.m. to R over Divisary Alarm at H.Q. A.S.P.I.C. from 38 Fd Amb.	AF
WARLOY	12/4/18	4 p.m.	Made a reconnaissance of the cellars in HENENCOURT to select a suitable site for an A.D.S. – Interviewed G.O.C. 114 Bde & Laber called at A.D.M.S.	AF
"	13/4/18		Proceeded to MILLENCOURT and A.D.M.S. Capt Bennett proceeded to HENENCOURT to interview Australians with a view to their thin A.D.S. A.H. & D.M.S. called re Bathe Establishment for changing clothing of men exposed to enemy gas.	AF

WAR DIARY
or
INTELLIGENCE SUMMARY.

(Erase heading not required.) O.C. 129 Fd Amb.

Army Form C. 2118.

129TH FIELD AMBULANCE.

Place	Date	Hour	Summary of Events and Information	Remarks and references to Appendices
WARLOY	14/4/18		Visited MILLENCOURT and BAIZIEUX. Called at Bde H.Q. ASMS & O.C. 131st Fd Ams called. Major Riddell returned. Capt Campbell & Capt Bennett made further reconnaissance of HENENCOURT for site suitable for A.D.S.	AJ
"	15/4/18		ADMS called. Capt of Varley returned from leave.	AJ
"	16/4/18		Capt D.S. Campbell C.A.M.C. proceeded to No. 3 Canadian Stationary Hospital for duty. Capt Bennett proceeded to HENENCOURT to establish an ADS on the ellows vacated by 114 Bde H.Q.	AJ
"	17/4/18		Attended Conference of O.C. Fd Ambces at ADMS Office. D.A. 2nd Lds called.	AJ
"	18/4/18		Visited ADS and Capt Varley.	AJ
"	19/4/18		Visited ADMS Office. Major Riddell made reconnaissance of HQRS from V24c 22 to HENENCOURT.	AJ
"	20/4/18		Further reconnaissance with Major Riddell of the area between MILLENCOURT and BOUZINCOURT. Attended Conference at ADMS Office. Conference of R.O. M.O's, A.D.M.S. & 131 held at this site to decide details of evacuation in the operations which are pending. Lieut D.B. Ruick (T.C) & Lieut B.G. Sharp (S.R) joined for duty. Additional Personnel of A.S.C. ASC joined for duty. Reconnoitred route to be employed in the evening of events this night.	AJ
"	21/4/18		At 7:30 p.m. the Left ½ of Bde attacked the German lines in front of BOUZINCOURT. The right Bn, which was being relieved by this unit, obtained posts farther in the attack. The wounded were carried from the Left Bn area by the bearers of 131st Fd Amb to V24c 22, from which point they were carried by bearers of this unit forth car post on the	AJ

WAR DIARY or INTELLIGENCE SUMMARY

Army Form C. 2118.

FIELD AMBULANCE

of 129 Fd. Amb.

Place	Date	Hour	Summary of Events and Information	Remarks and references to Appendices
WARLOY	22/4/18		SENLIS – HENENCOURT Rd. Cars cleared from here to the ADS at HENENCOURT & from there to the MDS at WARLOY. Proceeded to RAP at 7-30 p.m. – the first casualties arrived there about 9-45 p.m. Returned to MDS at 10-30 p.m. Clearance from the forward area was very rapid so it was possible to take cars along the track almost to V23d.1.6. After midnight, owing to the rain, the track would no longer stand by cars so had carriage by the SENLIS – HENENCOURT had to be adopted. About 4 a.m. on account of heavy rain the track became very difficult for cars to carry along so it was decided to clear from V24.C.2.2 along the road to MILLENCOURT when they were loaded into cars & clear via HENENCOURT. In order to facilitate clearing, instructions were sent up at 6 a.m. to clear road from the front to BOUZINCOURT where cars were sent & the remaining casualties were cleared by that route.	
"	23/4/18		Proceeded to RAP at 7 a.m. & found the clearance to be proceeding satisfactorily. At 10 a.m. all cases were clear & there were no further cases to be brought down from V24.C.2.2. A walking wounded post was established at V16.a.5.5. & 131 Fd. Amb. from which lorries cleared to WARLOY, but the majority of the walking wounded followed the trams & arrived the ADS HENENCOURT. The lorries were then dispatched to HENENCOURT. Over 170 walking wounded & 250 stretcher cases passed through the RAP.S. up to 9 a.m. There were all disposed of. MDS at WARLOY together with 80 walkers who passed through the post at V16.a.5.5.	

WAR DIARY
or
INTELLIGENCE SUMMARY
(Erase heading not required.) O.C. 129 Fd Amb

Army Form C. 2118.

FIELD AMBULANCE.

Instructions regarding War Diaries and Intelligence Summaries are contained in F.S. Regs., Part II. and the Staff Manual respectively. Title pages will be prepared in manuscript.

Place	Date	Hour	Summary of Events and Information	Remarks and references to Appendices
WARLOY	23/4/18		There were very few casualties from the right Bde. The proceeding of shells caps was unusually high & a very high proportion of wounds were of a severe nature. Which cases were cleared quickly. Many of local to M.O. & sight cases were always treated by M.Os medical transport to effect clearance.	
"	24/4/18		Visited ADS at 12 noon. Found all clear. Capt. Bennett returned to H.Q. Orders received that ADS & many posts will be taken over & brought by Australians. Proceeded to ADS to arrange details of relief. Battns at ADS. Lieut. Massey proceeded to TOUTENCOURT to take over cars required in Fd Amb of 63 Div. Major Rees to ADMS office to receive of orders. Three cars of Personnel wounded at HENENCOURT. Hamd Dressed. Relief of Personnel are postponed.	
	25/4/18		Lieut Massey Massey returned from TOUTENCOURT. ADMS called. Major Rebul Bapt. Ord. returned to ADS being relieved by Lieut. Massey. Delich.	
	26/4/18		Visited VADENCOURT to ascertain arrangements for relief. Some of called 3 also O.C. No 7 Australian Fd Amb. ADS & Foward posts returned by personnel from No 7 Australian Fd Amb. relief completed by 11 pm when Lieuts Massey Lich returned with all personnel & equipment	

Army Form C. 2118.

WAR DIARY
or
INTELLIGENCE SUMMARY.
(Erase heading not required.)

O.C. 129 Fd Amb.

Instructions regarding War Diaries and Intelligence Summaries are contained in F.S. Regs, Part II. and the Staff Manual respectively. Title pages will be prepared in manuscript.

Place	Date	Hour	Summary of Events and Information	Remarks and references to Appendices
WARLOY	27/4/18		Lieut Reith proceeded in lorry with 13th Bath (works) R.E. Visited HARPONVILLE with major Reitel to look in a Fd Amb site	AS
"	28/4/18		Capt Bennett proceeded to VADENCOURT with an advance party	AS
"	29/4/18		Unit moved to VADENCOURT and took over site from no 7 Australian Fd Amb. The sick at WARLOY handed over to a relieving party from no 7 Australian Fd Amb.	AS
VADENCOURT	30/4/18		Visited NAOURS. Conference of Ambulance Commanders at Adm.S office	AS

W. Thompson Col.
WDiv.S 38mDiv

Jones
Lieut Col
O.C. 129 Fd Amb

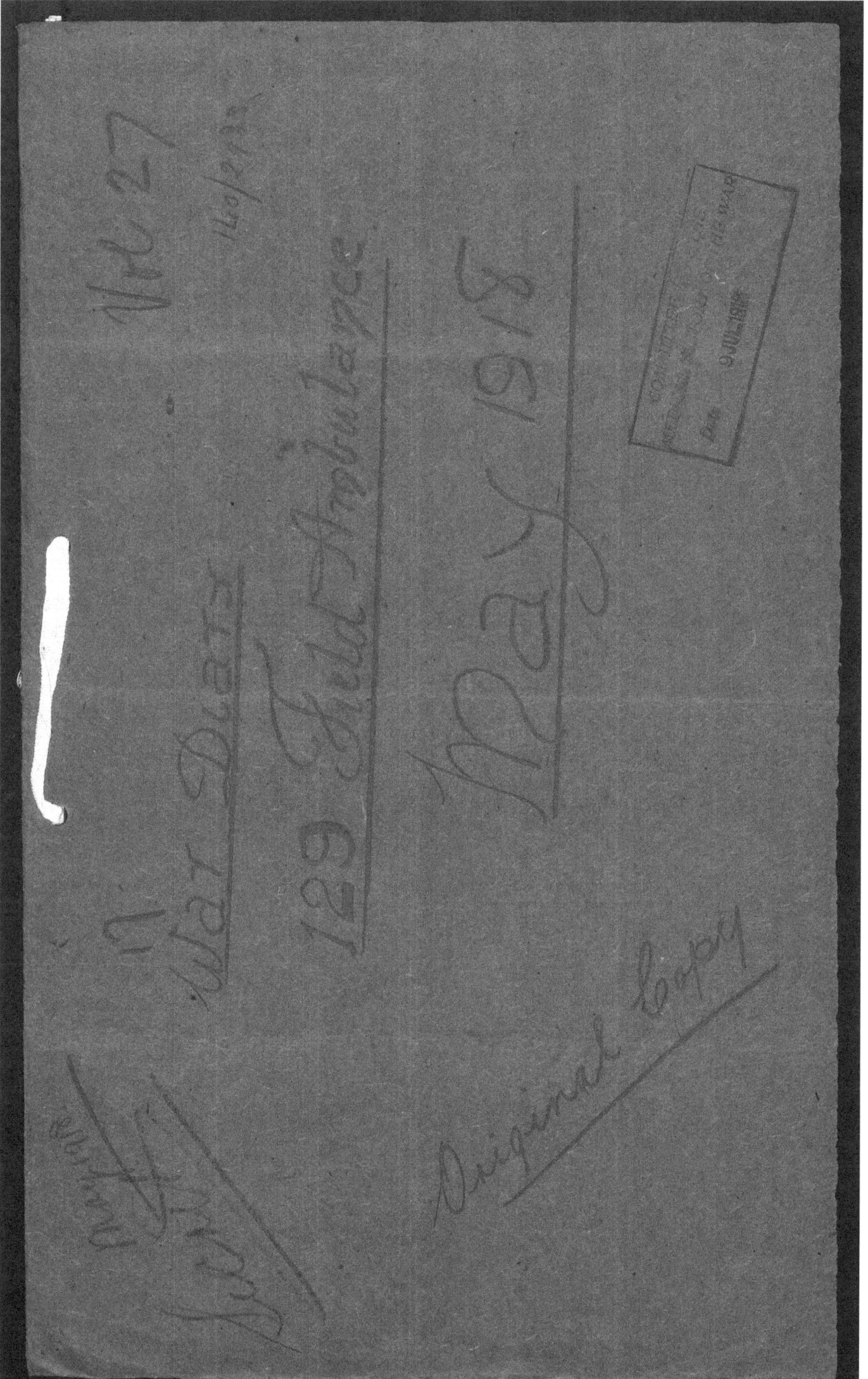

Vol 27

War Diary
129 Field Ambulance
May 1918

Original Copy

Army Form C. 2118.

WAR DIARY
or
INTELLIGENCE SUMMARY.

O.C. 129 Fd Amb

(Erase heading not required.)

Place	Date	Hour	Summary of Events and Information	Remarks and references to Appendices
VADENCOURT	1/5/18		Attended conference at ADMS office	
do	2/5/18		Took over channing BOUZINCOURT actn from 131 Fd Amb also area N of BOUZINCOURT from 105 Fd Amb	
do	3/5/18		Visited RAP's & ADS. with ADMS.	
do	4/5/18		ADMS & Corps inspected site	
do	5/5/18		Attended conference at ADMS office	
do	6/5/18	10 a.m.	Visited HAP. Chanina & forward area handed over to 131 Fd Amb. Unit moved to HARPONVILLE & encamped in a field. Attacking Station at VADENCOURT handed over to 45 London Fd Amb	
HARPONVILLE	do	2 p.m.	ADMS called	
do	7/5/18		Capt Bennett returned ADS to Lieut Sharp.	
do	8/5/18		ADMS called. Collected ADMS offr. 1st DW Morgan US. taken on strength	
do	9/5/18		Major J.F. Rees proceeded to England on expiry of contract. Capt Bennett, Lieut Innes & 150 Other Ranks dung proceeded to 131 Fd Amb for temporary duty. Major J.A. Bankie taken on the strength from 131 Fd Amb	
do	10/5/18		2 O.R. wounded & evacuated to CCS	
do	11/5/18		Major Bankie reported for duty. Capt Bennett, Lieut Innes & 150 Other Ranks returned. 1 O.R. wounded	
do	12/5/18		Lieut DW Morgan MO W.S R.C. struck off strength. Collected ADMS offr.	
do	14/5/18		Capt Bennett relieved Lieut Sharp at RAP SENLIS.	
do	15/5/18		Lieut O.R. + 2 Officers inspection	
do	16/5/18		ADMS called. 1 Lieut Christoffson U.S. R.C. joined for duty. Capt Bennett reported from ADS	

Army Form C. 2118.

WAR DIARY
or
INTELLIGENCE SUMMARY.

(Erase heading not required.) O.C. 129 Fd Amb.

Instructions regarding War Diaries and Intelligence Summaries are contained in F. S. Regs., Part II. and the Staff Manual respectively. Title pages will be prepared in manuscript.

Place	Date	Hour	Summary of Events and Information	Remarks and references to Appendices
HARPONVILLE	18/5/18		Pte L Douglas awarded Military Medal	
do	19/5/18		Lieut J. L. Bramhall (S.R.) joined for duty.	
do	20/5/18	10 am	Moved to CLAIRFAYE & took over ante from 131 Fd Amb. Capt Geo. B. Henry proceeded to American Army	
CLAIRFAYE		11 am	Capt E. J. M. Plumpt joined for duty	
do	21/5/18		Made a reconnaissance of BROWN LINE with Major Reid	
do	22/5/18		do — do — . Attended conference at some office	
	23/5/18		Majors I Capt Cullen inspected cars	
do			Made a reconnaissance of Brown Line with G.O.C. 114 Bde of Bde. Lt Christoffersen proceeded to 2nd RWF for duty.	
			The Headqrs. Orderly Cpls. accompanied by Ptes inspected the ambulance cars	
do	24/5/18		Selected sites for MDS, RAP. an cases of defensive fronture. Took census of persons remaining on brown line & noted for evacuation.	
			Proceeded with Bomb Officer & rounds the brown line. Capt Brown made reconnaissance of	
do	26/5/18		ENGELBELMER area	
do	27/5/18		Major Brookes, Capt Brandt made reconnaissance of PURPLE line	
			CLAIRFAYE. He advised by MO. A that TOUTENCOURT in case of emergency would be allotted to 120 Fd Amb for Colonel Gray — conveyed my answer to 3rd Army — or handed firmer	
do	28/5/18		Officers Kahn at 130 Fd Amb for instruction	
do	29/5/18		Inspected site done in connection Cranford for Bon Line	
do	30/5/18		Officer visited & selected site for Ros. at LEALVILLERS - TOUTENCOURT Rd	
do	31/5/18		Capt Short proceeded to 17 RWF for temporary duty. Called at 149 Fd Amb to arrange details for taking over tomorrow first.	

A.Cmd. Lieut Col. RAMC
OC 129 Fd Amb.

14

SECRET

War Diary. Vol 28
	160/3076.

129 Field Ambulance.

June 1918

June 1918.

129TH FIELD AMBULANCE.
No. 31
Date 6/18

Original Copy

Army Form C. 2113.

129TH FIELD AMBULANCE
No. ...... Date ....

WAR DIARY
or
INTELLIGENCE SUMMARY.
(Erase heading not required.)

OC 129 Fd Amb

Instructions regarding War Diaries and Intelligence Summaries are contained in F. S. Regs., Part II. and the Staff Manual respectively. Title pages will be prepared in manuscript.

Place	Date	Hour	Summary of Events and Information	Remarks and references to Appendices
CLAIRFAYE	1/6/18		Visited Reg Ad Posts & Adv Dressg Stations in ENGLEBELMER. Lects work at 149 Fd Amb.	AJ
"	4/6/18		AANS route site. Lieut B.B. Sharp struck off strength.	AJ
ENGLEBELMER	5/6/18	7.a.m	Proceeded to ENGLEBELMER with two cars to arrange details for taking over advance of the line A.D.S.	AJ
			Proceeded hence to relieve all the forward aid posts etc — relief completed by 11 a.m.	AJ
			Capt Bennett & Lieut Cranshill took over the ADS at HEDAUVILLE from O/C 149 Fd Amb.	AJ
"	6/6/18		Visited RAP's. Commenced to construct dugout shelters at ENGLEBELMER	AJ
"	7/6/18		do	AJ
"	8/6/18		Visited outposts with AANS	AJ
HEDAUVILLE	9/6/18		Took charge of RDS HEDAUVILLE. Capt Bennett proceeding to ENGLEBELMER A.D.S. Lt DeMay & Lt Crenshaw us no RC found for duty. DADMS called	AJ
CLAIRFAYE	10/6/18		Returned to HQ. Capt Plonghi proceeded to HEDAUVILLE for duty & Lt Crenshaw to ENGLEBELMER.	AJ
"	13/6/18		Lt Crenshaw returned to HQ. Proceeded DADMS to ADS ENGLEBELMER. Lt Crenshaw proceeded to HEDAUVILLE for duty.	AJ
ENGLEBELMER	14/6/18		Visited rug and posts.	AJ
do	15/6/18		AANS called with Major Bankes in morning. DADMS called in afternoon.	AJ
do	16/6/18		Visited RAP's & four personnel.	AJ
CLAIRFAYE	17/6/18		Returned to HQ. Major Bankes & Lt Crenshaw to ENGLEBELMER for duty. Capt Bennett returned to HQ.	AJ
"	18/6/18		14 reinforcements joined. Proceeded to ADS's and baths.	AJ

WAR DIARY
or
INTELLIGENCE SUMMARY
(Erase heading not required.)

Army Form C. 2118.

129th FIELD AMBULANCE

O.C. 129 Fd. Amb.

Instructions regarding War Diaries and Intelligence Summaries are contained in F.S. Regs., Part II. and the Staff Manual respectively. Title pages will be prepared in manuscript.

Place	Date	Hour	Summary of Events and Information	Remarks and references to Appendices
CLAIRFAYE	19/6/18		Visited ADMS Orchard	
ENGLEBELMER	20/6/18		Proceeded to ENGLEBELMER with Capt Bennett. Tried our route via Cultivé avenue. Found it impassable owing to the rain. Made a reconnaissance of the road tracks leading from MESNIL to VITERMONT. divided & clean grave along the road. Afterwards conferred ADMS Office & afterwards returned to ENGLEBELMER. Additional bearer arrived for operations. Major Riddell in charge at HEDAUVILLE.	
"	21/6/18	2 a.m.	Raid expected in enemy line. Casualties arrived at ADS at 4-30 a.m. The casualties were light considering the no. of men who took part in the raid (30 prisoners & 24 walking wounded). The evacuation of the load presented no difficulty & was speedily effected. Capt Plowright & Lt Amdrek returned to HQ. Lieut De May proceeded to HEDAUVILLE.	
CLAIRFAYE	"	11 am	Returned to H.Q. with Capt Bennett.	
"	22/6/18		Went to Church in TOUTENCOURT — LEAVILLERS. Rnd. ADMS called. Visited ADM Dressing Station. Major Banks returned from ENGLEBELMER.	
"	23/6/18		Major Banks proceeded to ADMS Office for temporary duty. Capt Bennett to HEDAUVILLE — Major Riddell & Lieut De May to ENGLEBELMER.	
"	24/6/18		Lt Crandal returned to H.Q.	
"	27/6/18		Major Banks reported from ADMS Office. ADMS inspected	
"	28/6/18		Visited ADM Dressing Station.	
"	29/6/18		Lt Crandel to HEDAUVILLE — Capt Bennett returning to HQ. ADMS inspected site. Approved conferring ADMS Office.	
"	30/6/18		AA & QMG inspected the site. Visited Advanced Dressing Station.	

AS James Lt Col
OC 129 Fd Amb

5339) Wt. W160/M3016 1,500,000 10/17 McA & W Ltd (E 1898) Forms W3091.   Army Form W.3091.

Cover for Documents.

Nature of Enclosures.

Notes, or Letters written.

ORIGINAL

WAR DIARY
of 129 Field Ambulance

From 1st July 1918
To 31st July 1918

129TH FIELD

Army Form C. 2118.

WAR DIARY
or
INTELLIGENCE SUMMARY.

(Erase heading not required.) O.C. 129 Field Ambulance

Instructions regarding War Diaries and Intelligence Summaries are contained in F. S. Regs., Part II. and the Staff Manual respectively. Title pages will be prepared in manuscript.

Place	Date	Hour	Summary of Events and Information	Remarks and references to Appendices
Sit on TOUTEN COURT	1/7/18		Visited A.D.S. & outposts	A.9
	2/7/18		Visited A.D.S. Capt Plowright to A.D.S. for duty.	A.9
LEALVILLERS ROAD	3/7/18		A.D.S. Major Bankes to A.D.S. ENGLEBELMER in relief of Major Riddell	A.9
do	4/7/18		Returned to H.Q. Hdqrs Office.	A.9
do	5/7/18		Lieut Crawshall to A.D.S. HEDAUVILLE in relief of Lt. Bomalrat	A.9
do	6/7/18		Visited 21st Div billets.	A.9
do	7/7/18		Proceeded to A.D.S. & made reconnaissance of HAMEL sector with Major Bankes for a scheme for a new road MESNIL-VITERMONT - no suitable spot found. Decided to continue the clearance along the Road.	A.9
	8/7/18		H.Qrs inspection kit. Major Riddell proceeds to A.D.S. to arrange the internment of civilian equipment.	A.9
do	9/7/18		Attended Conference at Hd.qrs Office with H.Qrs staff	A.9
do	10/7/18		Visited ADS ENGLEBELMER to arrange details for the clearing of wounded casualties.	A.9
do	11/7/18		Capt Bennett, Lieut Bomalrat & self proceed to A.D.S ENGLEBELMER, Major Riddell to ADS HEDAUVILLE. Raid made on enemy trenches in HAMEL Sectr by 2nd R.W.F. at 11 p.m. Major Bankes in charge of Bearers at MESNIL. Scheme worked smoothly - casualties (approx) 36 lying & 32 walking. 1 wounded prisoner. Germn soldrn reported by Capt Plowright at A.D.S. ENGLEBELMER in fair cond & suffering from shock.	A.9
do	12/7/18		Returned to H.Q. and Major Bankes & Capt Plowright. Stand ordered etc	A.9

Army Form C. 2118.

WAR DIARY
or
INTELLIGENCE SUMMARY.

(Erase heading not required.) O.C. 129 Fd Amb.

Instructions regarding War Diaries and Intelligence Summaries are contained in F. S. Regs., Part II. and the Staff Manual respectively. Title pages will be prepared in manuscript.

Place	Date	Hour	Summary of Events and Information	Remarks and references to Appendices
S.H. on TOUTENCOURT - "LEALVILLERS" ROAD.	13/7/18		ADMS called. Major Riddel moved forward station in relief of Lieut Crawfull. Capt Plowright visited ADS's & ascertain the condition of wounded whilst Padioux tried most firm - Found all were doing well.	
"	15/7/18		Conference Adms Office. Barnes & Dearne V Corps inspectors. Major Riddel returned from HEDAUVILLE.	
"	16/7/18		Major Riddel visited ADS's & later accommodation moved HQ to dirt spot. Various Adms Offrs.	
"	17/7/18		" ADS HEDAUVILLE	
"	18/7/18		" ADS ENGLEBELMER. Major Riddel proceeded to HERISSART to arrange for billets. ADS HEDAUVILLE handover to 17 Div - Lieut McKay & friends returned to HQ.	
HERISSART	19/7/18		Unit moved to HERISSART. Sits on TOUTENCOURT - LEALVILLERS Rd Landowners Adv party of 131 Fd amb. ADS ENGLEBELMER & Journal held handed over to 63rd Div - Capt Burnett & Journal returned to HQ. Lt Don proceeded for temporary duty with 142 Bde RFA. Capt Plowright & Lt Crawfull proceeded to ADS.	
do	20/7/18		Capt Vardy, Lieut Comstock, 72 OR & it Sure transport proceeded to VALHEUREUX to take over Dr Rd Station from 131 Fd Amb.	
do	22/7/18		Took over ADS from 131 Fd Amb. Vardy to SRP with ADMS. Lieut Crawfull & 17 OR remained at HERISSART - the rest of the Unit transfers to VALHEUREUX.	
VALHEUREUX	do		Three Halldon & Rfl Cunningham awarded Bar to MM	
do	25/7/18		Major Barber proceeded to Adv Hosp for duty. Three Halldon & Rfl Cunningham awarded Bar to MM General Hosp for duty. Capt Burnett to No 1 Australian. Lt Comstock to No 3 CCS for transfer in treatment of after.	

Army Form C. 2118.

WAR DIARY
or
INTELLIGENCE SUMMARY.

(Erase heading not required.) O.C 129 Fd Amb.

Instructions regarding War Diaries and Intelligence Summaries are contained in F. S. Regs., Part II. and the Staff Manual respectively. Title pages will be prepared in manuscript.

Place	Date	Hour	Summary of Events and Information	Remarks and references to Appendices
VALHEUREUX	26/7/18		sent off to Fild. Amb. called. Proceeded to HERISSART + arranged for the withdrawal of the personnel being duty there.	
do.	30/7/18		to Brandall Personnel returned to H.Q. from HERISSART. Some motor cars required reinforcement.	

Jones
Lieut Col RAMC
O.C. 129 Fd Amb

Vol 30
14g/3200.

SECRET

Aug 1918.

(ORIGINAL)

WAR DIARY

of

129 FIELD AMBULANCE

From 1st August 1918

To 31st August 1918

WAR DIARY
or
INTELLIGENCE SUMMARY.

(Erase heading not required.)

O.C. 129 Fd Amb

Army Form C. 2118.

Place	Date	Hour	Summary of Events and Information	Remarks and references to Appendices
VALHEUREUX	1/8/18		D.A.D.M.S. V Corps inspected estb. Lieut V L Crandall proceeded to 76th R.W.F. for duty. Lieut Crnather reported from 16.C.S.	AF
"	3/8/18		Lieut De Kay reported from 122 Bde R.F.A.	AF
"	4/8/18		Lieut Crnather proceeded for temporary duty with 17 R.W.F.	AF
"	5/8/18		G.O.C. 38 Div & A.D.M.S. called. Battle surplus arrived VALHEUREUX	AF
"	6/8/18		63 Buenos sent to 730 Fd Amb for duty.	AF
"	7/8/18		Attended Conference at A.D.M.S. Office. DDMS & DADMS called	AF
"	8/8/18		G.O.C. 38 Div visited estb. Lieut De Kay proceeded to 731 Fd Amb for temporary duty	AF
"	9/8/18		11 O.R. sent to 56 C.C.S. for duty	AF
"	10/8/18		Major Burkitt proceeded on leave	AF
"	11/8/18		ADMS inspected useful officers OR at DRS. DDMS V Corps inspected estb.	AF
"	13/8/18		Lieut De Kay rejoined from 131 Fd Amb	AF
"	14/8/18		A.S.V.D.M.S. visited estb.	AF
"	15/8/18		Lieut De Kay & 20 O.R. proceeded to 21 G.C.S. for temporary duty. Lieut Crnather rejoined. DADMS inspected estb.	AF
"	16/8/18		28559 Sgt Goldsmith promoted duty. 11 O.R. rejoined from 56 C.C.S	AF
"	17/8/18		Attended Conference at ADMS office. Major Ruttell proceeded and ratored to 73 Fd Amb	AF
"	19/8/18		Visited 131 Fd Amb	AF
"	20/8/18		ADMS called. 48022 Pte J Jones died of wounds at 56 Fd Amb. D.R.S. closed & patients on	AF
"	21/8/18		Jan'n' on forestalls.	AF
"	24/8/18		Moved to Quartière CLAIRFAYE relieved major Ruttell & had dinner rejoined	AF
CLAIRFAYE	25/8/18		DDMS called	AF

Army Form C. 2118.

WAR DIARY
or
INTELLIGENCE SUMMARY.

(Erase heading not required.) O.C 129 Fd Amb

Instructions regarding War Diaries and Intelligence Summaries are contained in F. S. Regs., Part II. and the Staff Manual respectively. Title pages will be prepared in manuscript.

Place	Date	Hour	Summary of Events and Information	Remarks and references to Appendices
CLAIRFAYE	26/8/18		Moved forward to Chateau HEDAUVILLE	
HEDAUVILLE	27/8/18		Roll called. 27858 Pte J.A. Elkington time exp H/Cpl, 101256 Pte J. Ireland now A/Cpl - Gen sythy. 42242 Pte J. Hunt - Sgt/A/S now temp H/Sgt. Brewed proms Offr & M.O. mentioned with OFFSTAFF of Divisn. Located job for Guarantee. Collected stray stamed/ 130 = 13: St Mathews. Dr Gradnor proceeded to 73 Rnf for temporary duty. Major Bowers returned from leave.	[sigs]
"	28/8/18			
"	29/8/18		Advance party sent to new site in ALBERT - BAPAUME Road. Unit moved to site in ALBERT-POZIERES Road near LA BOISELLE	
AT LA BOISELLE	30/8/18		ASRC called.	
"	31/8/18		Bomb & parade called. Roll called	

Hans Robb
Lieut
O.C 129 Fd Amb

129 Field Ambulance

Original

WAR DIARY.

for month of SEPTEMBER 1918

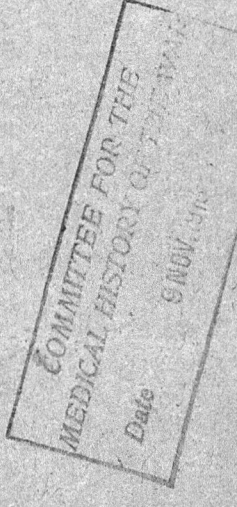

WAR DIARY / INTELLIGENCE SUMMARY

Army Form C. 2118.

OC 129 Fd Amb

Place	Date	Hour	Summary of Events and Information	Remarks and references to Appendices
LA BOISELLE	1/9/18		BOMS called. 48034 Pte Ridgeley & 48737 Pte Hy Whiting were stretcher suffering from dysentery evacuated whilst in duty as 21 CCS. 42241 Pte Wright — sore throat — to SEW at arm. 58534 Pte Sharp — wounded — advance in hospital.	
do	2/9/18		BOMS & POMS called. Visited ADMS office.	
do	3/9/18		Visited BEAULENCOURT — ordered out for Guards Div. Orders received from ADMS new Div CRA & Munro that unit moved to take over the BEAULENCOURT — WARLENCOURT Road relieved up to the reception of [wounded] cases. 48941 Pte R.S. Grimpton wounded "Graves"	
BEAULENCOURT	5/9/18		BMS & POMS & POMS motorcycle Handed over Bivouacks to 130 Fd Amb. Unit moved to BAZENTIN-LE-PETIT	
BAZENTIN	6/9/18		Ambulance conference at POMS office — decided that this Unit should clear the line when tel. from wind in. Hours to be May 7.16 or relieved from 21 CCS	
do	7/9/18		Called at POMS office	
do	8/9/18		POMS called	
do	9/9/18		Went north with Rds to ROC QUIGNY	
ROCQUIGNY	10/9/18		Proceeded to FINS ADS to ascertain system of evacuation of [wounded] officers & wounded forwarded to FINS at 3 pm to clean mid ADS.	
do	11/9/18			

Army Form C. 2118.

WAR DIARY
or
INTELLIGENCE SUMMARY.
(Erase heading not required.)

Place	Date	Hour	Summary of Events and Information	Remarks and references to Appendices
FINS	11/9/18		Took over the various Reg and Bn posts & took over the manning of the line - relief completed at 7 p.m.	
do	12/9/18		when preparatory move to FOUR WINDS FARM. 10.15 a.m. made an attack on the enemy trenches - operation specially planned.	
			Moved Regt Bn Posts on the right front with Major Rickett Capt Prichard & Lt Boyd. B.30 to a Bn attacked & performed duty.	
do	13/9/18		Moved Regt Bn Posts on the left with Major Buckell W.M. & Lieuts Collis, Head Bn advanced all. Head Bn to a side near ETRICOURT W. Reports enemy withdrawing.	
do	14/9/18		Moved Regt Bn Posts sharpe W.M. & Lieut Collis. Bn & B.H.Q's inspected the Reg Bn Posts in company with O.C. Heavy enemy shelling of camp & company at 8.45 a.m. a number of the other Coy men 48.311 Sergt E.E. Jones killed & 48673 Sgt Lindsay wounded.	
do	15/9/18		10 am. changed fry of platoon of Bn. Reported affair to Major Rickett & inform he	
do	16/9/18		9 a.m. moved all our Posts with us at 9. Major Rickett & advance the forward and had to be left front near COUZEAUCOURT with Co. H. partly between enlisted & concluded this the majority of the unit. Orders were changed and to operate speedily opened troops had not arrived this Coy mounted up at apt Rickett & sides and as this never EQUANCOURT but decided not to which part until tomorrow night.	

WAR DIARY
or
INTELLIGENCE SUMMARY.

(Erase heading not required.)

OC 129 Fd Amb

Place	Date	Hour	Summary of Events and Information	Remarks and references to Appendices
FINS	10/9/18		Visited 113 FdS HdQrs & have provided to Lt/Col aux Post Stretcher nobles & groundsmen with MO's of 113 Bde	
do	17/9/18		Visited Reg aid Posts — made full preparations for the change of treatment of heavy casualties, bombs & drums called. Visited three Infantry Bde. at work. Walked cannot on all sectors between FINS & EQUANCOURT. OC 131 Fd Amb made preparations for relationship to broken wounded Post arranged for the Fd Amb sectors. 4 & 2) Staff Sgts have wounded MO M	
do	18/9/18	5:30 am	Attack opened in enemy trenches by 113 & 114 Bdes in conjunction with other Divisional troops. Relief provided to Rt aid Post of Major Bowker & the left ruin Ruin. All cars damaged in 15 minutes repaired with the exception of one Just. Stretcher called & approx. 1/2 hour Ambulance sometimes from accordingly. near EQUANCOURT.	
		6:30am	Parties provided to carry forth on the right sectors one Care the sent up at once - provided to left sector & three stretchers from Advance Party stretcher provided. 6 parties to Rt aid & three stretchers of ambulance cars & drivers called & Heard of being enough but 6 cars into 2 cars to tarmac Advanced P.O.T. 6 cars removed.	
		8 pm	All returned 6 cars returned work 6 cars into 2 cars & track Advanced P.O.T. Home and from 83 FW. Engineer at new return.	
		9:30 pm	Provided R at Rt Aid Posts, and the returned and run excellently - no complaints O delays at any R Posts. Parties to left aid Posts. Few cases have come	

WAR DIARY
or
INTELLIGENCE SUMMARY.

(Erase heading not required.) O.C. 129 Fd Amb

Army Form C. 2118.

Place	Date	Hour	Summary of Events and Information	Remarks and references to Appendices
F I N S	18/9/18	dawn	Position of Before 1/13 Bde prevented Turns Fd assistance from Bde that the left had been taken	
"	18/9/18	3 pm	Returned to Fins - everything found satisfactory	
			At the gaps around all the Turns on stretch - large numbers were passing through. 45 German wounded passed through	
		4 pm	No difficulty in dealing with the wounded - Germans now coming down. No Nos 17 & 21 SAC's called. Took our stretcher in running from left hand arm & drove a slightly slightly wounded Turkey's gun Reipel of attack to the made thought we knew each other.	
		7 pm	The staff came down to the elimens were -	
			① The attendants I attending these Signals of Bands heard say no - he was down before he asked - so strongly between in future Shortens	
			② The wheatarms came as unformed as possible - the enemy did not heavily shell the main road during the day time & some came clear from forward any part	
			③ To arrange a C.C.P to APP where several streams are met - had one short as the wounded to clear line to M.D.	
			④ To have a large moving shelter at the ADS - this gr/ from the most necessary when the line was company standing of arms to clear	

bar

Army Form C. 2118.

WAR DIARY
or
INTELLIGENCE SUMMARY.

(Erase heading not required.) O.C. 17.9 F. Amb

Instructions regarding War Diaries and Intelligence Summaries are contained in F.S. Regs., Part II. and the Staff Manual respectively. Title pages will be prepared in manuscript.

Place	Date	Hour	Summary of Events and Information	Remarks and references to Appendices
FINS	19/9/18		Visited Aid Posts. Major Roberts & Major Bradie returned to A.D.S. Major M.H. Greenshields, Major through A.D.S. belonging to 17 Div. Collected Blts. Advance party of 52 Fd. Amb. arrived.	J.H.
	20/9/18		Moved own H.Q. to 52 Fd. Amb. & sent away to ROCQUIGNY	J.H.
ROCQUIGNY	21/9/18		Took over N.R.S. run by BEAUENCOURT from 130 Fd Amb.	J.H.
BEAUENCOURT	22/9/18		Handed over charge of N.M.I. Major Russell & provided on 14 days leave.	J.H.
"	22/9/18		Took over charge of unit. 1/ Lieut G.A. DEMPSEY U.S. H.O.R.C. proceeded to take over medical charge of 1/19th Welch Regt. (Pioneer) 48036 Sergt (A/SI Sergt) B Thomas R.A.M.C. awarded bar to military medal. 8814. Pte B.G. Philbrick R.A.M.C. awarded military medal.	See
"	23/9/18		D.D.M.S. inspected site. 48804. Pte D.S. OWEN, R.A.M.C. evacuated to C.C.S. – sick. Capt. J. Purtie H.E. R.A.M.C. (S.R.) and Lieut L.M. Moore R.A.M.C. (T.C.) joined for temporary duty from 131 Field Ambulance.	See
"	24/9/18		A.D.M.S. visited. W.D/4 069494 Pte J. DAVIES APC AT attached, evacuated sick to C.C.S.	See.
"	25/9/18		D.A.D.M.S. visited. 90965 Pte A.J. Tozer R.A.M.C. evacuated sick to C.C.S.	See.

Army Form C. 2118.

WAR DIARY
or
INTELLIGENCE SUMMARY.
(Erase heading not required.)

Instructions regarding War Diaries and Intelligence Summaries are contained in F. S. Regs., Part II. and the Staff Manual respectively. Title pages will be prepared in manuscript.

Place	Date	Hour	Summary of Events and Information	Remarks and references to Appendices
Beaufrent	26/9/18		D.A.D.M.S. called. Two additional Nissen huts erected at D.R.S.	Sun.
"	27/9/18		Attended conference held by G.O.C. Division. Tactical situation explained. Conference with A.D.M.S. & O's. C. 130 & 131 Field Ambulances.	Sun.
"	28/9/18		Unit accompanied by transport marched to site near HEUDECOURT and came under orders of 113 Brigade. Unit at an hour's notice to move. Capt. Plunkett R.A.M.C. & detachment of 18 R.A.M.C. personnel left to run D.R.S. One horse ambulance left ADMS to evacuate cases to C.C.S.	Sun.
			A 8799. Pte W. Lewis R.A.M.C. awarded military medal. Capt. J. Purdie M.C. R.A.M.C. and Pte L.M. Moss R.A.M.C. reported from 131 Field Ambulance. The latter proceeded on transport duty.	
HEUDECOURT.	29/9/18		1 N.C.O. & 3 squads R.A.M.C. bearers attached to each battalion of 113 Brigade. 1 N.C.O. & 2 squads R.A.M.C. bearers attached to Brigade H.Q. 30 bearers returned from 16 R.W.F. Relieved Beaufrency duty as bearers. Evacuating sick of Brigade to S.P. count. Visited A.D.M.S. & G.O.C. Brig.	Sun.

Army Form C. 2118.

WAR DIARY
or
INTELLIGENCE SUMMARY.
(Erase heading not required.)

Place	Date	Hour	Summary of Events and Information	Remarks and references to Appendices
HEUDECOURT	29/9/18.		Visited Brigade H.Q. Made reconnaissance of HEUDECOURT - PERIERE area for suitable site for a M.D.S. There is a very good site on South side of Railway Embankment between HEUDECOURT & PERIERE. Arranged for transport of walking wounded by light railway from HEUDECOURT to FINS.	Seen
"	30/9/18.		35 Bearers from 114th & 113th Regt. reported for stretcher duty. Visited Brigade.	Seen

Signed
Major Ranee
O/C 129 Field Ambulance

W.S. Thompson Col.
ADMS. 38th Div.
30/9/18

129TH FIELD AMBULANCE

No. 1

ORIGINAL

Vol 3
WO/3401
38th Division

WAR DIARY
of
129 Field Ambulance
for month of October 1918

129th FIELD AMBULANCE
31-10-18

WAR DIARY
or
INTELLIGENCE SUMMARY.

Army Form C. 2118.

O.C. 129 Field Ambce

Place	Date	Hour	Summary of Events and Information	Remarks and references to Appendices
HEUDICOURT	1/10/18		Visited 113 Brigade H.Q. A.D.M.S. visited. Unit parked and at one hour's notice to move. Visited R.A.P's.	Gen.
"	2/10/18		Visited Brigade. A.D.M.S. visited. D.R.S at Beaulencourt.	Gen.
"	3/10/18		Visited Brigade & A.D.M.S. A.D.M.S ordered unit to move with 113 Brigade to EPEHY. Transport was split into two groups. The mobile group consisting of 1 water cart, 2 limbers, 2 G.S. wagons & 1 Horsed Ambulance wagon proceeded to Advanced Transport lines on South side of railway near PEIZIERES. The remainder of Transport remained at old site in charge of Quartermaster. Equipment necessary to run a Main Dressing Station was carried in Horsed Ambulance wagon. Unit marched to EPEHY arriving 7.30 pm.	Gen.
EPEHY	4/10/18		A.D.M.S. & D.A.D.M.S. visited. 16 R.A.M.C. O.R. & 4 bearers loaned as additional stretcher bearers to 131 Field Ambulance. Unit remain parked. Clearing sick of brigade. Unit early to be inspected. D.R.S. at Beaulencourt closed and personnel rejoined. Capt Alderidge R.A.M.C. I/c O.R. R.A.M.C. remains with Reception Centre to carry out individual appraisals.	Gen.
"	5/10/18		Transport lines moved to EPEHY, and refernte sites time allotted to A.D.B. Gotham. A.D.M.S. visited. Visited 131 Field Ambulance. Visited A.D.M.S. office. Reconnoitred roads leading from EPEHY to VENDHUILE, HONNECOURT. Horsed Ambulance from B.P.S. rejoined Transport.	Gen.

WAR DIARY or INTELLIGENCE SUMMARY

Army Form C. 2118.

O.C., 129 Field Ambulance

Place	Date	Hour	Summary of Events and Information	Remarks and references to Appendices
EPEHY	6/10/18		Opened Main Dressing Station. 11 wounded admitted — one died. Cases evacuated by 2 attached cars of 29 H.A.C. New Ford car received to replace Ford car evacuated to base. Under instructions from A.D.M.S., reconnoitred VILLERS-GUISLAIN & HONNECOURT for suitable site for M.D.S. One good site in former village occupied by Ambulance of 21st Division. No suitable site in latter village. Visited R.A.P.'s	Sun.
"	7/10/18		Visited Reception Camp. 6.1.8.12. At DARLING H RAM C. wounded evacuated to C.C.S. from 4pm all casualties from forward area are to be evacuated to combined M.D.S. near BANTEUX. Capt. & Mr T. Vowley R.A.M.C. proceeded to England on 14 days leave. 29 sick and 30 wounded (of which one died) passed through M.D.S.	Sun.
"	8/10/18		At 5.30 a.m., casualties both walking and lying, began to arrive from forward area in large numbers. Two cars of 29 H.A.C. were attached at the time. Evening sedan car lying wounded was immediately opened out to full capacity, and a separate building was organised to deal with walking wounded. Despatch rider was sent off immediately to 29 M.A.C. requesting 6 additional ambulance cars and lorry for walking wounded. Major Bond, was placed in charge of walking wounded and Capt Parlie M.C. in charge of stretcher cases.	Sun.

Army Form C. 2118.

WAR DIARY
or
INTELLIGENCE SUMMARY.
(Erase heading not required.)

O.C. 12g Field Ambulance

Place	Date	Hour	Summary of Events and Information	Remarks and references to Appendices
EPEHY	8/10/18	(cont.)	There were the only two officers attached to the unit at the time. Cases continued to arrive in large numbers and, as evacuation was rather handicapped from time to time by the shortage of M.A.C. cars, two standing beds were fitted to accommodate cases waiting evacuation. To diminish congestion, unit cars were used to evacuate to C.C.S. Shortly after 9am urgent request for all available cars to clear forward area was received from O.C. 131 Field Ambulance. Two large cars were sent immediately and 1 large and 1 Ford were sent immediately on return from C.C.S. This temporarily increased congestion but shortly after 8am. 6 M.A.C. cars arrived and evacuation to C.C.S. at YTRES proceeded smoothly. Lorry for walking wounded did not arrive and walking wounded, after being dressed, fed, rested, were conveyed to FINS by empty ammunition lorries. Three horsed ambulances were also employed to evacuate to this A.D.S. D.D.M.S. visited site. H.Q. officer visited Stretcher cases, and walking wounded continued to arrive in large numbers until mid-day. After midday, for stretcher cases were brought in owing to the rate of evacuation being changed to evacuate M.D.S. near Bantouy. Walking wounded continued to arrive in empty lorries until about 3.30pm. All stretcher cases were cleared by 1pm and all W.W. shortly after 3.30pm. During that time, 4 off. sick and 402 wounded handled, of which 4 wounded died at the dressing station, 19 officers and 365 O.R. belonged to 38th Divn. 5 wounded German prisoners were also passed through.	Sun.

WAR DIARY
or
INTELLIGENCE SUMMARY.

(Erase heading not required.)

Army Form C. 2118.

O.C. 129 Field Ambulance

Instructions regarding War Diaries and Intelligence Summaries are contained in F. S. Regs., Part II. and the Staff Manual respectively. Title pages will be prepared in manuscript.

Place	Date	Hour	Summary of Events and Information	Remarks and references to Appendices
EPÉHY	8/10/18	Cont'd	Most of the stretcher cases were very severely wounded, while the walking wounded had exceptionally slight wounds. Men's both lying & walking were cleared & passed through A.D. Posts. All stretcher cases received A.T.S. D.D.M.S. visited site. A.D.M.S. visited site at 4pm & gave orders to close down. M.A.C. cars were instructed to report to M.D.S. Barleux. Received orders from A.D.M.S. to proceed on following day to site near RANCOURT FARM & to march with T/4 G16.9797 Lt. T. Davis A.E.M.T. rejoined from C.C.S.	Sn.
EPÉHY	9/10/18		Reconnoitred site for M.D.S. and fixed on RANCOURT FARM. Unit accompanied by transport moved at 6.30am to this site, arriving 9am. At 3 p.m. received orders to reconnoitre VILLERS-OUTREAUX. Site unsuitable for M.D.S. and Unit to proceed thro' forthwith. Officer's Reccé was fixed on in the next suitable building and Harnessers to be accommodated in the MAIRIE. Unit arrived at 5pm? 5 Rank. O.R. reinforcements formed Guard. Party was starting of division from midnight 19-10-15 ist. Order received to open up "M.D.S. for 38 & 33 Division by 8 am following day. 13 sick & 5 wounded from 131 field ambulance. MAC cars returned	Sn.

A 0092 Wt: W1128.9/M1293. 750,000. 1/17. D D & I Ltd. Forms/C2118/14.

Army Form C. 2118.

WAR DIARY
or
INTELLIGENCE SUMMARY.

O.C. 129 Field Ambulance

(Erase heading not required.)

Instructions regarding War Diaries and Intelligence Summaries are contained in F. S. Regs., Part II. and the Staff Manual respectively. Title pages will be prepared in manuscript.

Place	Date	Hour	Summary of Events and Information	Remarks and references to Appendices
VILLERS-OUTRÉAUX	10/10/18		Opened as M.D.S. at 8am. Orders received from A.D.M.S. to reconnoitre CLARY for site suitable for M.D.S. Tried as German reservation but of unite church, and upholstering party. Close. One section proceeded as advance party. H.D.M.S. visited. Closed as M.D.S. at 3pm and unit accompanied by transport proceeded to CLARY	Jen.
CLARY	11/10/18		Capt T.W. MELHUISH R.A.M.C. 130 & Field Ambulance attached (ophthalmic duty). 95436, Pte B. Woolbrook R.A.M.C. evacuated C.C.S. "Gas shell wound" suffering ache and too intensely transports located in CLARY have numbers of civilians suffering from influenza to be attended. A.D.M.S. and D.A.D.M.S. called. Clerk attached for duty. to establish M.D.S (33 + 38 D initions) at CLARY. Pte 344 Pte C. Rigby R.A.M.C. evacuated C.C.S. Gas shell wound. 58534 Pte J Thorpe " 6583 " G. Knox " Reconnoitred TROIS-VILLES for site suitable for M.D.S. and fixed in School.	Jen.
CLARY	12/10/18		Orders received from A.D.M.S. to take over advance site at BERTRY from 131 Field Ambulance. Unit accompanied by transport arrived at new site at 2pm. A.D.M.S. called. One shelling of village. 15 O.R. of 14th R.W.F. arrived wounded as result of direct hit on billet, of whom, one died.	Jen.

Army Form C. 2118.

WAR DIARY
INTELLIGENCE SUMMARY.
(Erase heading not required.)

O.b. 129 Field Ambce

Place	Date	Hour	Summary of Events and Information	Remarks and references to Appendices
BERTRY	13/10/18		Capt J. Purdie M.C. RAMC proceeded on temporary duty at Embrie M.D.S. of 33 & 38th Divisions at CLARY. Motor car attached to 131 field Ambulance for temporary duty.	See
"	14/10/18		Additional clerk detailed for duty at Embrie M.D.S. Clary. H.Q.M. recalled. Clerk from 131 field Ambulance attached for temporary duty. Capt J. Purdie RAMC rejoined unit.	See
"	15/10/18		Conference at ADMS office. Two clerks withdrawn from M.D.S. Clary. Proceed to M.D.S. Montigny. Two clerks of 131 field Ambulance, Clerk from 131 field Ambulance detached for temporary duty rejoins own unit. Visited M.D.S. Montigny.	See
"	16/10/18		Reoccupied INCHY forsite suitable for M.D.S. Ecole des filles is a possible likely is being shelled. Capt Purdie M.C. RAMC & 2 additional RAMC personnel to Corps Hair Dressing Station MONTIGNY for temporary duty. Lieut. T. Innes RAMC returned from leave and resumed command of unit.	See

Army Form C. 2118.

WAR DIARY
INTELLIGENCE SUMMARY.
(Erase heading not required.)   O.C. 129 Fd Amb

Instructions regarding War Diaries and Intelligence Summaries are contained in F. S. Regs., Part II. and the Staff Manual respectively. Title pages will be prepared in manuscript.

Place	Date	Hour	Summary of Events and Information	Remarks and references to Appendices
BERTRY	17/10/18		Major Entwistle assumed MO	JA
"	18/10/18		Capt Plunkett & personnel rejoined from 38" Dw Reception camp. A.D.M.S. called.	JA
			Preparations made for further shift & reception of walking wounded.	JA
"	19/10/18		Wounded commenced to arrive at 5.30 am. Total of 220 cases passed through, including 27 P.O.W.	JA
"	20/10/18		Major Reid proceeded on leave to U.K.	JA
			Lieut R.A. Moore Rums Dove over to FCoS	JA
			ADMS called	JA
"	21/10/18		Reconnoitred for Amb site at MONTAY but no suitable one obtained.	JA
"	22/10/18		Found a ruinous conv convent and FOREST for a site - a suitable roads in factory	JA
"	23/10/18		to bury mud is a Adv of 33 Dw Visited Corps WW Pod at INCHY. Proceeded	JA
"	24/10/18		forward as to do organization	JA
"	25/10/18		Transferred to FOREST. Took over dressing station from 19 Fd Amd	JA
FOREST	26/10/18		Hostile bombing called	JA
"	27/10/18		ADMS 3rd Div 0 aidpots & recommend useful in. ADMS called.	JA
			Large amount of supplies in the ruinous billets & burg cleared away. Flys nuisance very bad.	JA
"	28/10/18		Offered Corps HQrs at mess for the reception of lying cases evacuated from forward BAS at INCHY. Arrangements ordey including 6 cyt Buick (129 Fd Amd) 5 cyt	JA

W.L. W1128.g/M4293. 750,050. 1/17. D.&D & I. Ltd. Forms/C2118/24.
A.7092

WAR DIARY

INTELLIGENCE SUMMARY

O.C. 129 Fd Amb

Place	Date	Hour	Summary of Events and Information	Remarks and references to Appendices
FOREST	29/10/18		Staff returns called. Capt J McLyn/ Smith duty. Doanven unit the rate of w.w. but further aspect in a Beamry.	
"	30/10/18		Advance Corps moved at 17.00 hours & moved to the Beamry. Stood unto orders received. Preparations made to adapt site for the reception of military wounded.	
"	31/10/18		Maj Baker proceeded to the Corps W.W. post at INCHY for instruction. Stood unto orders received. No advance Corps reported sick.	

Jones
Lt Col RAMC
OC 129 Fd Amb

98/33
14/2401

SECRET

Nov 1918

ORIGINAL WAR DIARY
of
129 FIELD AMBULANCE
for month of November 1918.

WAR DIARY
or
INTELLIGENCE SUMMARY.
(Erase heading not required). O.C. 129 F Amb.

129TH FIELD AMBULANCE

Place	Date	Hour	Summary of Events and Information	Remarks and references to Appendices
FOREST	1/11/18		ADMS called. Capt Purdie proceeded to 14th RWF. Major Bankes reported from INCHY.	
"	2/11/18		Opened at 3 p.m. for the reception of walking wounded. Tel: Takeover of 104 F Amb found impossible duty. Attended conference at ADMS office	
"	3/11/18		ADMS called	
"	4/11/18		Operations commenced at 5-30 a.m. Walking wounded began to arrive at 9 a.m. in steady stream passed through throughout the day. Clearance effected until 1 a.m. Wounded admitted up to midnight :-	

```
                    Officers      O.R.  356
         17 Div                     9
         21  "                      4
         33  "                    259
         38  "           10        67
         Other Foreign              55
         P of W           1       ---
                        ---       750
                 Total   25
```

"	5/11/18		100 sick admitted & returned overnight. ADMS accompanied by DDMS & ADMS inspected site. Evacuated 120 F Amb returned to this unit. Capt Plowright proceeded to temporary duty to C of o. MDS	

WAR DIARY
or
INTELLIGENCE SUMMARY.

(Erase heading not required.)

O-C 129 Fd Amb.

Army Form C. 2118.

129TH FIELD AMBULANCE.

Place	Date	Hour	Summary of Events and Information	Remarks and references to Appendices
FOREST	1/11/18		Appns called. Capt Purdie proceeded to 1/4 RWF, Major Barker reported from INCHY.	
"	2/11/18		Opened at 3 pm. In the reception of walking wounded. Established of 107 Fd amb. found in temporary duty. Attended conference at Adms office	
"	3/11/18		Stand to called	
"	4/11/18		Operation commenced 5-30 am Walking wounded began to arrive at 9 am. Fr steady stream from thence to Thornhill & day. Advance section went forwd.	
			Wounded admitted up to midnight :-	
				Officers	OR		
			17 Div	92	356		
			21 "	1	9		
			33 "	1	4		
			38 "	10	259		
			Other formations		67		
			P.of.W	1	55		
			Total	25	750		
	5/11/18		100 such admitted & retained overnight Ams reinforcements OSRMS + RSTRS in-patient site. Removed 13.0 Fd amd admn arrived. Capt Plowright proceeded to temporary duty to 63rd FdAS	

WAR DIARY
INTELLIGENCE SUMMARY

129TH Field Ambulance

Army Form C. 2118.

Place	Date	Hour	Summary of Events and Information	Remarks and references to Appendices
FOREST	6/11/18		ADMS called. Major Banks proceeded with DDMS to find a site near LOCQUIGNOL	
"	7/11/18		Proceeded to LOCQUIGNOL to inspect arrangements for FWCP	
"	8/11/18		Proceeded with advance party to LOCQUIGNOL to open up for reception of W.W.	
LOCQUIGNOL			Opened up at 2 pm. 5 shake down dressing station at FOREST. ADMS called	
"	9/11/18		ADMS called	
"	10/11/18		Major Banks proceeded to BERLAIMONT to select a site for walking wounded — no suitable one discovered.	
"	11/11/18		Cessation of hostilities at 11 am. Received confirmation that Capt A.H.T. Daniels would return us to the command of the unit. Capt Davies assumed command. Handed over command to Capt A.H.T. Daniels RAMC. 65 F. Amb. Proceeded to ENGLAND for	
"	12/11/18		demobilization. Took over command of no 129 Field Ambulance yesterday from Capt (A/Lieut Col) A Jones D.S.O. MC RAMC under authority from ADMS 3rd Army. Conference at a DMS Office yesterday. Traced Divisional Rest Station Inc. at 8 a.m. DDMS called yesterday. Major Gloag MC RAMC Thorgan Cuthn RN returned from the unit yesterday. Returned all personnel	

WAR DIARY
or
INTELLIGENCE SUMMARY.

Army Form C. 2118.

AMBULANCE

O.C. 129 Fd. Amb.

Instructions regarding War Diaries and Intelligence Summaries are contained in F. S. Regs., Part II. and the Staff Manual respectively. Title pages will be prepared in manuscript.

Place	Date	Hour	Summary of Events and Information	Remarks and references to Appendices
Locquinol	14.11.18	—	O.Mo. Fld. Ambulance & Corps to our side today. A.D.M.S. called. Fine bright day - frost at night -	JWB
"	15.11.18		Very bright day - frost at night - Major Riddel returned from leave today -	JWB
"	16.11.18		R.S.T. by cold day. Very heavy frost all night. Capt. PURDIE reported from temporary duty as P.M.O. to R. Welsh Fusiliers -	JWB
"	17.11.18		A. & D.M.S. visited. Returned all Corps Walking Wounded Tent & Latrines -	JWB
"	18.11.18		A.D.M.S. & D.A.D.M.S. visited. Returned all surplus Medical Stores & Equipment. Rain descended after at CAMBRAI - Weather changed to-day - at about 4.30 pm. Saw Stars & overcast -	JWB
"	19.11.18		Three motor trucks to-day -	JWB
"	20.11.18		Nil -	JWB
"	21.11.18		D.A.D.M.S. Corps visited - Capt. PLOWRIGHT departs for ENGLAND and ordered to report to War Office on arrival	JWB
"	22.11.18		Orders received for CAPTAIN PURDIE RAMC to report to ADMS 42nd Division -	JWB
"	23.11.18		Orders received of CAPTAIN PURDIE RAMC cancelled - CAPTAIN MACINTYRE R.A.M.C. received orders from A.D.M.S. 32 Div. Report to A.D.M.S. 32nd Division -	JWB
"	24.11.18		CAPTAIN MacINTYRE left to report to A.D.M.S. 32nd Division - MAJOR RIDDEL departed on leave granted from 26.11.18 to 26.12.18 -	JWB
"	25.11.18		Nil -	JWB
"	26.11.18		Nil -	JWB

WAR DIARY
or
INTELLIGENCE SUMMARY.

O.B. 129 3rd Bn

Place	Date	Hour	Summary of Events and Information	Remarks and references to Appendices
Locquignol	9/11/18		Nil -	
	10/11/18		Very wild weather - a good deal of rain -	
	11/11/18		Nil -	
	12/11/18		Much colder today. Slight frost last night.	

J.D. Dunn
Lt Col Comme

12q FIELD AMBULANCE

ORIGINAL
WAR DIARY
for
month of DECEMBER 1918.

Army Form C. 2118.

WAR DIARY
or
INTELLIGENCE SUMMARY.
(Erase heading not required.)

O.B. 129 Field Ambulance

Instructions regarding War Diaries and Intelligence Summaries are contained in F.S. Regs., Part II. and the Staff Manual respectively. Title pages will be prepared in manuscript.

Place	Date	Hour	Summary of Events and Information	Remarks and references to Appendices
Locquinol	1.12.18		A.D.M.S. visited – I proceeded to new area to arrange site and accommodation for Field Ambulance. I fixed on the village of FRANVILLERS, being most central position in Brigade area – and offering the most suitable accommodation – viz the village school and adjoining buildings. It had previously been used as site for Field Ambulance.	
"	2.12.18		Returned from FRANVILLERS, leaving a holding party of 1 N.C.O. & two men there to start getting the site in order.	
"	3.12.18		HIS MAJESTY the KING visited the Divisional area – Special Parade of 1 Officer & 70 men representing the FIELD AMBULANCE – proceeded to ALNOYE.	
	4.12.18		Move to new area postponed probably until after Xmas.	
	5.12.18		CAPTAIN L./cpl. IVAN DAVIES.R.A.M.C. reported for duty – and taken on the Strength from 4.12.18.	
	6.12.18		Orders received for 35 miners to be prepared to leave for CAMBRAI on 8. Inst.	
	7.12.18		Orders re. 35 miners altered – 14 only now required.	
	8.12.18		14 miners leave for CAMBRAI for reference.	
	9.12.18		Nothing to report.	
	10.12.18		Captain L/cpl IVAN DAVIES M.C. R.A.M.C. reported to O.C. 19th R.W.Fusiliers to proceed as M.O./c. transport as far as new area.	
	11.12.18		Nothing fresh.	
	12.12.18		Nothing fresh.	

Army Form C. 2118.

WAR DIARY
or
INTELLIGENCE SUMMARY.

(Erase heading not required.)

O.C. 129 Field Ambulance

Instructions regarding War Diaries and Intelligence Summaries are contained in F. S. Regs., Part II. and the Staff Manual respectively. Title pages will be prepared in manuscript.

Place	Date	Hour	Summary of Events and Information	Remarks and references to Appendices
Locquinil	13.12.18		CAPTAIN. J. PURDIE M.C. R.A.M.C. admitted to 4 C.C.S. with Jaundice – CAPTAIN HERBERTSON R.A.M.C. reported from 38th D.A.C. for temporary duty –	AAA
"	14.12.18			
"	15.12.18			
"	16.12.18			
"	17.12.18			
"	18.12.18		Between these dates there was nothing to note	AAA
"	19.12.18			
"	20.12.18			
"	21.12.18			
"	22.12.18			
"	23.12.18			
"	24.12.18			
"	25.12.18		Christmas Day – cold frosty day – nothing to note	AAA
"	26.12.18			AAA
"	27.12.18		Transport leaves for new area – CAPTAIN HERBERTSON R.A.M.C. in machine transport charge of 113 Brigade transport until arrival at new area.	AAA
"	28.12.18		Personnel of 129 Field Ambulance leaves LOCQUINOL & arrives at INCHY –	AAA

Army Form C. 2118.

WAR DIARY
or
INTELLIGENCE SUMMARY.
(Erase heading not required.)

O.C. 129 Field Ambulance

Instructions regarding War Diaries and Intelligence Summaries are contained in F. S. Regs., Part II. and the Staff Manual respectively. Title pages will be prepared in manuscript.

Place	Date	Hour	Summary of Events and Information	Remarks and references to Appendices
INCHY	29.12.18		Personnel leaves INCHY by bus 9 arrives at WARLOY -	AAA
WARLOY	30.12.18		Take over the Hospice WARLOY as site for the Field Ambulance -	AAB
" "	31.12.18		TRANSPORT arrived at 11 a.m. - MAJOR BANKES proceeds on leave from 1.1.19 to 15.1.19 -	AAC

M.O. Davis
Lieutenant

38 DIV Box 2356

129 FIELD AMBULANCE 9/81 35

Original
WAR DIARY
for month of JANUARY 1919

129th FIELD AMBULANCE

Army Form C. 2118.

WAR DIARY
or
INTELLIGENCE SUMMARY.
(Erase heading not required.)

O.C. 129 Field Ambulance

Place	Date	Hour	Summary of Events and Information	Remarks and references to Appendices
WARLOY	1.1.19		Field Ambulance still situated in the "Hospice" at WARLOY.	A.D.S.
	2.1.19		Nothing to report.	A.D.S.
	3.1.19		Nothing to report	A.D.S.
	4.1.19		6 O.Ranks 238 Employment Company proceeded to Camp Commandant 38th Division and	A.D.S.
			were struck off strength. D.D.M.S. Corps & A.D.M.S. 38th Div. visited.	A.D.S.
	5.1.19		Nil report.	A.D.S.
	6.1.19		Nil report	A.D.S.
	7.1.19		Nil report	A.D.S.
	8.1.19		Nil report	A.D.S.
	9.1.19		Nil report	A.D.S.
	10.1.19		Nil report.	A.D.S.
	11.1.19		Three other ranks proceeded to dispersal area for demobilization.	A.D.S.
	12.1.19		Visited A.D.M.S. Office. CAPTAIN A.C. WILSON RAMC(T) joined for temporary duty from	A.D.S.
			121 Bde R.F.A.	A.D.S.
	13.1.19		Ten other ranks proceeded to dispersal area for demobilization.	A.D.S.
	14.1.19		One other rank proceeded to dispersal area for demobilization.	A.D.S.
	15.1.19		Two other ranks proceeded to dispersal area for demobilization.	A.D.S.
	16.1.19		Nothing to report.	A.D.S.
	17.1.19		Nothing to report	A.D.S.
	18.1.19		Two other ranks proceeded to dispersal area for demobilization.	A.D.S.

Army Form C. 2118.

WAR DIARY
or
INTELLIGENCE SUMMARY.
(Erase heading not required.)

O.C., 129 Field Ambulance

Instructions regarding War Diaries and Intelligence Summaries are contained in F. S. Regs., Part II. and the Staff Manual respectively. Title pages will be prepared in manuscript.

Place	Date	Hour	Summary of Events and Information	Remarks and references to Appendices
WARLOY	19.1.19		Two Other Ranks proceeded to dispersal area for demobilization	M.D.
"	20.1.19		One Other rank proceeded & dispersed area for demobilization	M.D.
"	21.1.19		One Other rank proceeded to dispersed area for demobilization	M.D.
"	22.1.19		Two Other ranks proceeded to dispersal area for demobilization. Major G.W. RIDDEL granted extension of leave to 15.1.19. - Major J.H. BANKES granted extension of leave to 23.1.19.	M.D.
"	23.1.19		Major J.H. BANKES RAMC. rejoined from leave.	M.D.
"	24.1.19		Release of Officers & Other Ranks of Maintenance and Administrative Services & Pioneers curtailed by leave of department concerned	M.D.
"	25.1.19		Major J.H. BANKES RAMC proceeded to HQRs. 38th DIV. to take up the duties of D.A.D.M.S.	M.D.
"	26.1.19		/Lieut G.A. DE MAY M.S. M.O.R.C. joined for duty	M.D.
"	27.1.19		Three Other ranks reported for duty from R.A.M.C. Base Depot	M.D.D.
"	28.1.19		A.D.M.S. visited - Nine Other ranks taken on strength	M.D.
"	29.1.19		Nothing to report -	M.D.
"	30.1.19		Under orders A.D.M.S. 38th Div. /Lieut G.A. de May RAMC U.S. M.O.R.C. reported for duty as M.O. i/c 13th Punjab Motor Section.	M.D.S.
"	31.1.19		Nothing to report.	M.D.S.

W.L. Sampson
Col
A.D.M.S. Div
Alderson

A7092 Wt. W1125 9/M1293 750,000. 1/17. D.D. & L. Ltd. Forms/C2118/14.

129 Field Ambulance

Original

War Diary

for

month of February 1919

Army Form C. 2118.

WAR DIARY

INTELLIGENCE SUMMARY.

(Erase heading not required.)

O.C. 129 Field Ambulance

Place	Date	Hour	Summary of Events and Information	Remarks and references to Appendices
WARLOY	1.2.19		The Officers, rank proceeded to dispersal area - A New Year's Honours Gazette 1919 - Rewards for service in the field - The following were the awards made in respect of the Field Ambulance - the O.B.E. to Lieutenant Colonel J. YARLEY R.A.M.C. - "O.B.E." No 48010 A/Q.M.S. S.O. GARRETT R.A.M.C. D.S.M. No 48040 Pte J. WILLIAMS R.A.M.C. Mentioned in Despatches.	O/c & RAMC A/ Q.M.S. D.S.M.
"	2.2.19		Nothing to report	N.D.S.
"	3.2.19		Two Other ranks R.A.M.C. proceeded to dispersal area.	N.D.S.
"	4.2.19		D.A.D.M.S. visited - D.A.D.V.S. visited & classified horses for demobilization	N.D.S.
"	5.2.19		Visited MONTIGNY to ascertain site for the Field Ambulance	N.D.S.
"	6.2.19		Visit of H.R.H. the Prince of WALES - the Officers and men paraded with	N.D.S.
"	7.2.19		Visit Ebert Farm to choose site for Field Ambulance - MAJOR G.W. RIDDEL M.C. R.A.M.C. returned from leave.	N.D.S.
"	8.2.19		Q.M.S. GARRETT & S/Sgt THOMAS & Pte DOUGLAS proceeded to dispersal area.	N.D.S.
"	9.2.19		MAJOR BANKES R.A.M.C. struck off strength 18.1.19 on proceeding to take over duties D.A.D.M.S. 38th Welsh Division.	N.D.S.
"	10.2.19		Proceeded on leave for 14 days from 11.2.19 to 25.2.19 - Handed over temporarily to MAJOR G. RIDDEL M.C. R.A.M.C.	N.D.S.

A.D. Dun
Lt.Col R.A.M.C

Army Form C. 2118.

WAR DIARY
or
INTELLIGENCE SUMMARY.
(Erase heading not required.) O.C. 129 Field Ambulance

Instructions regarding War Diaries and Intelligence Summaries are contained in F. S. Regs., Part II. and the Staff Manual respectively. Title pages will be prepared in manuscript.

Place	Date	Hour	Summary of Events and Information	Remarks and references to Appendices
Warloy	10/2/19		Took over charge of unit during absence on leave of Lt. Col. A.H.T. Davis R.A.M.C. A.D.M.S visited unit and made their farewell on this leaving division to assume duties of D.D.M.S 8th Corps.	Sgd. Map ref.
"	11/2/19.		One R.A.M.C. N.T. granted special leave to U.K.	Sgd.
"	12/2/19.		One L.D. "Y" horse returned to unit from Army Collecting Station having been claimed by owner as favourite horse.	Sgd.
"	13/2/19.		2. O.R's proceeded [ ] information that 1 N.C.O. and 3 men had been demobilised whilst on leave in U.K. 73931, Pte. H. Standen. R.A.M.C. proceeded to report to D.M.S. Third Army for temporary duty as clerk.	Sgd.
"	14/2/19.		Nothing to report	Sgd.
"	15/2/19.		3. O.R. R.A.M.C. left for demobilization 86014, Pte L.W. Jones, R.A.M.C. transferred to 38th D.H.Q. for duty Attack of Influenza	Sgd.

Army Form C. 2118.

WAR DIARY
or
INTELLIGENCE SUMMARY.

(Erase heading not required.)

O.C., 129 Field Ambulance

Place	Date	Hour	Summary of Events and Information	Remarks and references to Appendices
Bailey	16/2/19		Capt. R.E. WILSON, R.A.M.C. proceeded 15/2/19 to 127 Brigade R.F.A. to take over medical charge of R.A.	Pen.
"	17/2/19		Nothing to report.	Pen.
"	18/2/19		Nothing to report. except visit of Col. Bateman, D.P.O., R.A.M.C. ADMS 38th Division.	Pen.
"	19/2/19		Eight Z. Horses sent to V.E.S. MONTIERES to be sold at Amiens on 22nd inst.	Pen.
"	20/2/19		1. O.R. R.A.M.C. left (demobilization). 4 O.R. R.A.M.C. proceeded to report to O.C. 41 Stationary Hospital for temporary duty as nursing orderlies. 3 O.R. R.A.M.C. with 6 new establishment transferred to 38th Divisional Train - strength of unit.	Pen.
"	21/2/19		48686 Pte. R. Hicklenough R.A.M.C. granted special leave to U.K. 21/2/ to 7/2/19. 70 R proceeded for demobilization.	Pen.

Army Form C. 2118.

WAR DIARY
or
INTELLIGENCE SUMMARY.
(Erase heading not required.)

O.C. 129 Field Ambulance

Instructions regarding War Diaries and Intelligence Summaries are contained in F. S. Regs., Part II. and the Staff Manual respectively. Title pages will be prepared in manuscript.

Place	Date	Hour	Summary of Events and Information	Remarks and references to Appendices
Wardrecques	22/2/19		3 O.R. proceeded for demobilization. 1 retainable Rank O.R. transferred to 130th Field Ambulance. 6 other Ranks received in exchange. 1 O.R. A.S.C. M.T. received in exchange. One driver A.S.C. M.T. evacuated.	See
"	23/2/19		Nothing to report	See
"	24/2/19		Conference at A.D.M.S. office.	See
"	25/2/19		12 A.D. "Z" horses transferred to No. 5 V.E.S. MONTIÈRES. 6 mules at Amiens. 1 O.R. (clerk) proceed to D.D.M.S. V Corps for temporary duty. Visit by G.O.C. Division.	See
"	26/2/19		Lt.-Col. Davis returned from leave.	See
"	27/2/19		Handed over to Lt.-Col. Davis commanding unit. Signed Major R.A.M.C.	See

Army Form C. 2118.

WAR DIARY
or
INTELLIGENCE SUMMARY.

(Erase heading not required.)

O.C. 129 Field Ambulance

Instructions regarding War Diaries and Intelligence Summaries are contained in F. S. Regs., Part II. and the Staff Manual respectively. Title pages will be prepared in manuscript.

Place	Date	Hour	Summary of Events and Information	Remarks and references to Appendices
WKR LOY	28.2.19		No boat. Pte C. W. Turner R.A.M.C. proceeded to A.D.M.S. office for temporary duty as clerk — A.D.M.S. & DA.DMS visited —	100 tem.
				100 tem. Influenza

129 Field Ambulance.

Original War Diary

for

month of March 1919

On His Majesty's Service.

O.C.
129TH FIELD AMB.

Army Form C. 2118.

WAR DIARY
or
INTELLIGENCE SUMMARY.
(Erase heading not required.)

O.C, 129 Field Ambulance

Place	Date	Hour	Summary of Events and Information	Remarks and references to Appendices
WARLOY BAILLON	1.3.19	—	No 418523 Pte D.H. LLOYD R.A.M.C. struck off strength on proceeding to report to O.C. 41 Stationary Hospital for duty as dispenser as from 27.2.19.	A.D.M.S. Divn.
"	2.3.19	—	Six other ranks proceeded for demobilization — Nothing to report.	1st Pte Rhone A.D.M.S.
"	3.3.19	—	No 12199 Pte A.G. PERRY R.A.M.C. struck off strength as from 16.11.18 having been demobilized from hospital in England — One L.D. "Y" horse sent Bonetta Camp on route for sale in England — Nothing to report.	A.D.M.S. A.D.M.S.
"	4.3.19	—	1 N.C.O. & 3 men proceeded to proposed new site at LAMOTTE BREBIERE as billeting party. —	A.D.M.S.
"	5.3.19	—	CAPTAIN W. HERBERTSON R.A.M.C. proceeded to U.K. for demobilization —	A.D.M.S.
"	6.3.19	—	Went to new site at LAMOTTE BREBIERE —	A.D.M.S.
"	7.3.19	—	Nothing to report.	A.D.M.S.
"	8.3.19	—	Sick other ranks proceeded for demobilization — One H.D "X" horse sent to Bonetta Camp —	A.D.M.S.
"	9.3.19	—	Horse Transport vehicle sent to Corps Park at LONGEAU —	A.D.M.S.
"	10.3.19	—	CAPTAIN L. of IVAN DAVIES R.A.M.C. struck off strength on transfer to 19 C.C.S. —	A.D.M.S.
"	11.3.19	—	Nothing to report.	A.D.M.S.
"	12.B.19	—	Nothing to report.	A.D.M.S.
"	13.3.19	—		A.D.M.S.
"	14.3.19	—	G.O.C. 38th Div visited to bid farewell on leaving the Division — 4 "Z" horses proceeded to Abbeville sale on 15th.	A.D.M.S.

Army Form C. 2118.

WAR DIARY
or
INTELLIGENCE SUMMARY.

(Erase heading not required.)

O.C. 129 Field Ambulance

Instructions regarding War Diaries and Intelligence Summaries are contained in F.S. Regs., Part II. and the Staff Manual respectively. Title pages will be prepared in manuscript.

Place	Date	Hour	Summary of Events and Information	Remarks and references to Appendices
WARLOY BAILLON	15.3.19	—	A.D.M.S. & D.A.D.M.S. visited – 6 O.R.s proceeded for demobilization –	A.D.M.S. Instr. 15/3/19
"	16.3.19	—	Visited new site at LAMOTTE BREIERE –	A.D.D.
LAMOTTE BREIERE	17.3.19	—	Moved here to-day. Holding party left at WARLOY-BAILLON – A.D.M.S. 38th Division left. J. Dainey D.A.D. R.A.M.C. acting A.D.M.S.	A.D.D.
"	18.3.19	—	Take over medical & sanitary charge of CADRES at BLANGY-TRONVILLE – 15th WELSH at LA NEUVILLE. Nothing at CORBIE –	A.D.D.
"	19.3.19	—	Nothing to report –	A.D.D.
"	20.3.19	—	Visited 15th RWFusiliers – & checked medical & surgical equipment under orders A.D.M.S. –	A.D.D.
"	21.3.19	—	2 H.D. "X" horses proceeded to I Corps Horse Camp –	A.D.D.
"	22.3.19	—	Acting A.D.M.S. & D.A.D.M.S. visited – Midwives Wilson Scott from WARLOY-BAILLON.	A.D.D.
"	23.3.19	—	Nothing to report –	A.D.S.
"	24.3.19	—	Nothing to report –	A.D.S.
"	25.3.19	—	Visited 131 Field Ambulance –	A.D.D.
"	26.3.19	—	Nothing to report	A.D.D.
"	27.3.19	—	Seven Officials Rank and File R.A.M.C. H.T. proceeded to different areas for demobilization	A.D.D.
"	28.3.19	—	MAJOR G.W. RIDDEL M.C. R.A.M.C. proceeded to report to O.C. 2nd R.L. Chorlton at BLANGY-TRONVILLE for duty as M.O. i/c troops that were struck off strength on June 29.3.19	A.D.D.

Army Form C. 2118.

WAR DIARY
or
INTELLIGENCE SUMMARY.
(Erase heading not required.) O.C. 129 Field Ambulance

Instructions regarding War Diaries and Intelligence Summaries are contained in F. S. Regs., Part II. and the Staff Manual respectively. Title pages will be prepared in manuscript.

Place	Date	Hour	Summary of Events and Information	Remarks and references to Appendices
LAMOTTE BREBIERE	29.3.19		Visited S. M.O's Office GUERRIEU.	1990.
"	30.3.19		W/3527 Ambulance Cars 200 1545 & 1528 proceeded to 38th Div M.T.C° for Transfer to	1990.b.
"	31.3.19		R.R.P. Nothing to report.	1993.

A.D.M.S.
Val Rame

129 FIELD AMBULANCE

Original

WAR DIARY

for month ending APRIL 1919

Army Form C. 2118.

WAR DIARY
or
INTELLIGENCE SUMMARY.
(Erase heading not required.)

129TH FIELD AMBULANCE.

Instructions regarding War Diaries and Intelligence Summaries are contained in F. S. Regs., Part II. and the Staff Manual respectively. Title pages will be prepared in manuscript.

O.C., 129 Field Ambulance

Place	Date	Hour	Summary of Events and Information	Remarks and references to Appendices
LAMOTTE BREBIERE	1.4.19		CAPTAIN G.W. RIDDEL M.C. R.A.M.C. relinquishes rank of Acting Major. Resumes of the strength of this unit.	A.D.M.S. 2nd Corps
"	2.4.19		CAPTAIN J.H. BANKES R.A.M.C. taken on the strength in from 29.3.19. No 823442 Pte J. HOELL R.A.M.C. struck off strength as from 28.1.19 on admission to hospital sick in U.K.S. Kingdom whilst on leave. 2 O.R's proceeded for demobilization. 30.3.19.	A.D.M.S.
"	3.4.19		Hon. Captain & Quartermaster J. VARLEY O.B.E. R.A.M.C. proceeded on leave U.K. for 14 days. O.C. 28th Div. Train visited & inspected Animal Accounts.	A.D.S.
"	4.4.19		No 41622 Pte J. VICKERS R.A.M.C. evacuated Att Stationary Hospital 'sick' Nothing to report	A.D.S.
"	5.4.19		CAPTAIN J.H. BANKES R.A.M.C. proceeded to I Corps S.T.P. as M.O. for I. Corps.	A.D.S.
"	6.4.19		3 O.R's R.A.M.C. proceeded for demobilization.	A.D.S.
"	7.4.19		6 O.R's R.A.S.C. M.S. T.P.B. non attached - proceeded to report H.Q. 38th Div. Train at Josephe Beacke. S.M.O. visited - 1st Lieut G.A. de MAY A.S.M. O.R.C. struck off strength	A.D.S.
"	8.4.19		Nothing to report	A.D.S.
"	9.4.19		Nothing to report	A.D.S.
"	10.4.19			A.D.S.

Army Form C. 2118.

WAR DIARY
or
INTELLIGENCE SUMMARY.

(Erase heading not required.) O.C. 129 Field Ambulance

Instructions regarding War Diaries and Intelligence Summaries are contained in F. S. Regs., Part II. and the Staff Manual respectively. Title pages will be prepared in manuscript.

129TH FIELD AMBULANCE

Place	Date	Hour	Summary of Events and Information	Remarks and references to Appendices
LAMOTTE-BREBIERE	11.4.19		Nothing to report –	A.D.Ms.
"	12.4.19		Nothing to report –	A.D.Ms.
"	13.4.19		3 O.R's R.A.M.C. proceeded to the base on Demobilization –	A.D.Ms.
"	14.4.19		3 O.R's R.A.M.C. proceeded to 41 Stationery Hospital for Company duty –	A.D.Ms.
"	15.4.19		2 O.R's R.A.M.C. struck off strength and proceeding on transfer to 41 Stationery Hospital –	
"		No 93331 Pte Stowell R.A.M.C. evacuated to Base "sick" on 11.4.19		A.D.Ms.
"		No 27998 Pte Tolmont R.A.M.C. struck off strength on transfer to Corps of M.M.Police 17th Div.		A.D.Ms.
"	16.4.19		Nothing to report –	A.D.Ms.
"	17.4.19		No 10204 Pte A Bush evacuated to Base "sick" struck off strength –	A.D.Ms.
"	18.4.19		Nothing to report –	A.D.Ms.
"	19.4.19		Nothing to report –	A.D.Ms.
"	20.4.19		No 439568 Pte J Silley R.A.M.C. granted special leave to U.K. to 4.5.19 –	A.D.Ms.
"	21.4.19		Nothing to report –	A.D.Ms.
"	22.4.19		Nothing to report –	A.D.Ms.

Army Form C. 2118.

WAR DIARY
or
INTELLIGENCE SUMMARY.

(Erase heading not required.) O.C. 129 Field Ambulance

Instructions regarding War Diaries and Intelligence Summaries are contained in F.S. Regs., Part II. and the Staff Manual respectively. Title pages will be prepared in manuscript.

129th FIELD AMBULANCE

Place	Date	Hour	Summary of Events and Information	Remarks and references to Appendices
LAMOTTE BRÉBIÈRE	23.4.19		Nothing to report —	app.
"	24.4.19		No 97082 Pte B.L. ANDREWS R.A.M.C. struck off strength on being taken to the North Mid. 141 Stationary Hospital —	app.
"	25.4.19		Capt. & Quartermaster J. YARLEY R.A.M.C. reported from leave — No 3147 Pte A. PALMER R.A.M.C. granted 14 days leave to France —	app.
"	26.4.19		Nothing to report —	app.
"	27.4.19		Nothing to report —	app.
"	28.4.19		Nothing to report —	app.
"	29.4.19		Nothing to report —	app.
"	30.4.19		Nothing to report —	app.

A.D. Devin
Lt Colonel.

Vol 39.
Censored

140/55/60

129 Field Ambulance

ORIGINAL WAR DIARY for month of MAY 1919

129TH FIELD AMBULANCE.

28031 W3125/M2250 1000m 6/17 M.R.Co.,Ltd. (1367) Forms W3091 Army Form W.3091.

BILLETING

Cover for Documents.

Nature of Enclosures.

Notes, or Letters written.

Army Form C. 2118.

12ᵗʰ Field Ambulance

WAR DIARY
or
INTELLIGENCE SUMMARY.
(Erase heading not required.)

Instructions regarding War Diaries and Intelligence Summaries are contained in F. S. Regs., Part II. and the Staff Manual respectively. Title pages will be prepared in manuscript.

Place	Date	Hour	Summary of Events and Information	Remarks and references to Appendices
LAMOTTE BREBIERE	1.5.19		No 374431 Sergt Major A BOLLAND struck off strength from 26.4.19. Having been evacuated sick to H1 Veterinary Hospital.	S.S.O. Div. Division
"	2.5.19		Nothing to report	M.O.D.
"	3.5.19		Nothing to report	M.O.D.
"	4.5.19		Nothing to report	M.O.D.
"	5.5.19		Court of Inquiry on illegal absence of Pte WALKER RAF MT ate 13ᵗʰ Field Ambulance	M.O.D.
"	6.5.19		Nothing to report	M.O.D.
"	7.5.19		Nothing to report	M.O.D.
"	8.5.19		Nothing to report	M.O.D.
"	9.5.19		Nothing to report	M.O.D.
"	10.5.19		Orders received cutting down cadre to 8 officers 444 O.Ranks	M.O.D.
"	11.5.19		Nothing to report	M.O.
"	12.5.19		T/CAPT G. W. RIDDEL M.C. R.A.M.C. proceeded to demobilization	M.O.
"	13.6.19		4 O.R. R.A.S.C. MT surplus to cadre Transferred to No 336 C R.A.S.C. BLANGY-TRONVILLE	M.O.
"	14.5.19		Nothing to report	M.O.
"	15.5.19		2 H.D. "Z" horses Transferred to C.R.A. 38ᵗʰ Division – Animals account chargé	M.O.
"	16.5.19		6 R.A.S.C. M.S. O.Ranks proceeded to report D.O.C. 30ᵗʰ Div. Train Kinhurt not cadre of 38ᵗʰ Division for England. 3 O.R. R.A.M.C. proceeded to report to O.C. 13ᵗʰ held Regt for some purpose.	M.O. 10.40.

Army Form C. 2118.

WAR DIARY
or
INTELLIGENCE SUMMARY.

(Erase heading not required.)

129 Field Ambulance

Instructions regarding War Diaries and Intelligence Summaries are contained in F. S. Regs., Part II. and the Staff Manual respectively. Title pages will be prepared in manuscript.

Place	Date	Hour	Summary of Events and Information	Remarks and references to Appendices
LAMOTTE BREBIERE	16.5.19		30 O.R.'s Rame proceeded to I Corps Concentration Camp - SAVEUSE for demobilization -	A.D.M.S
"	17.5.19		Trekked tonopied equipment handed in to No 34 Adv Base Medical Stores - POULAINVILLE -	M.O.D.
"	18.5.19		Nothing to report - Took over duties of S.M.O. 38th Div group Parker on 17.5.19 Capt A.J. Sparks Rame	A.D.M.S
"	19.5.19		Ordnance equipment handed in to I.O.O POULAINVILLE - Ford Sunbeam Ambulance sent to Div Reception Park	A.D.M.S.
"	20.5.19		Visited S.M.O I Corps group Parker & M.S. No 3 Green - Allotment received for 8 men to proceed to Corps Reception Camp - on 22.5.19	M.O.D.
"	21.5.19		Sergt Major B. Evans & 4 O.R's R.A.S.C. transferred to 38th Divisional Train -	M.O.D.
"	22.5.19		Sergt Watt & Corp Hulme & 3 O.R's R.A.S.C. M.T. transferred to Div M.T. Reception Camp - Hamelin - One motor cycle & one ambulance car damaged sent to same place - One motor cycle to VERT GALAND. Q.M.S. LAWRENCE & 4 O.R's Rame and to I Corps Reception Camp - Hon Capt & Quartermaster J. VARLEY O.B.E. R.A.M.C. evacuated to No 41 Stationary Hospital - No 129 Field Ambulance cease to exist as a Unit. Proper account handed in - Clearance certificate received from Field Cashier AMIENS.	M.D.

A.D. Owin
Capt Rame
O.C. 129 Field Ambulance